Beginning PHP & MySQL Development: Code Your Own Dynamic Website Today

1st Edition

Contents

Chapter 1: Introduction

In this chapter, we will discuss about different technologies used for building dynamic websites. This chapter will be a general overview of key components which are related to web development. We will begin with the common scenario of browsing a website, which will lead to the discussion of what happens under the hood when we try to access a website over Internet. We will briefly discuss about Web Servers, Hyper Text Markup Language (HTML), Cascading Style Sheets (CSS), Server Side Programming Language and Database. The goal is to give you a general understanding of how all these components fit together to produce a website.

The Client-Server Scenario

Let's start our discussion with the common scenario of browsing a website. Let's say you want to visit a website. Typically you will open your browser, enter the URL of the website to your favorite web browser's address bar and then you will hit Enter button. In a few seconds, you will be presented with the website on your web browser. I am sure you all know this part, but have you ever wondered how things are working in the background? In this section, I will attempt to explain the process.

What Goes On Behind the Scene?

Ok, the following description is going to be a bit long, but hang in there! As soon as you enter the address of the website in the browser's address bar and press 'Enter', your web browser will try to communicate with the computer where the website is hosted. You shouldn't be surprised to know that websites are stored in computers. These computers are usually special ones with powerful and hi-configuration hardware components. We call those computers "server computers" or servers for short. The web browser will try to communicate with the server. In case of computer to computer communication over a network (in this case, over Internet), the computers are identified by an IP address. An IP address is basically a numerical label assigned to each computer connected to a network. But how do you know the IP address of the website which you are trying to visit? The IP address of server computer will be obtained from its domain name. The domain name entered to the address bar of web browser will be translated to an IP address using a DNS (Domain Name Services) Server, usually this DNS server is hosted by your ISP (Internet Service Provider). Using this IP address, your web browser will communicate with the server where the website is hosted. Your browser will make an HTTP (Hyper Text Transfer Protocol) request to the server and the server will respond with a HTTP response, which will be sent back to your web browser who will interpret the HTTP respond and finally, you can see the website.

So you can see that, your browser makes a request and the server sends a response. This request-response process involves two parties, your web browser and the server. Your browser is sending the request for the website. We call the web browser a 'client' (Just like clients in real life who requests for products or services). On the other hand, the server which hosts the website listens to the incoming request and serves the content accordingly (thus its name, server!). The server computer will have a running process which intercepts the incoming requests and send corresponding responses. We call this running process which responds to requests the "web server".

Websites are hosted on server computers. Your web browser communicates with the server by using the IP address obtained from a website's domain name and making a HTTP request to the server.

Overview of Key Technologies

Now we will have a look at the major technologies related to web development. This is just to give you an idea about what they are and how they fit together to produce modern day 'dynamic' websites. Note that when we say dynamic, it does not refer to the website's appearance, but rather we say that in contrast to a static website whose content doesn't change according to user input e.g. your own homepage. A dynamic website's content changes dynamically based on user input e.g. Amazon or a blog.

Web Server

Web server is a software that runs on a server computer. It helps to deliver web pages accessed through the Internet. The web server listens to any incoming request by the client and responds to those requests accordingly. If its a successful request, the web server will respond with the requested resource (usually the web pages), else it will respond with an error message. The communication between client and server takes place through the HTTP protocol. (Protocol is just another 'hi-fi' word for 'rule' or 'process')

In early days, websites were typically static files consisting of HTML pages. But modern day websites often use server side programming languages (like PHP, Python, Ruby, ASP, Java etc), which can generate dynamic HTML files on-the-fly. Most web servers has support for these server side programming languages. So if any client requests for a dynamic web page, the web server will call the corresponding server side programming language for processing and the resulting HTML will be generated by the server side programming language which will be sent to the client.

A web server is a software which runs on a server computer and responds to HTTP requests sent by browsers from client computers.

HTML

HTML stands for Hyper Text Markup Language. HTML defines the structure of the web pages. HTML is a markup language, which consists of different tags. The different tags define parts of the website, like heading, paragraph, list, table, form etc. The HTML files are interpreted by web browsers. Take a look at very simple HTML file below:

```
<html>
    <head>
        <title>Hello</title>
    </head>
    <body>
        <p>Hello Guest! Thanks for visiting our website!</p>
    </body>
</html>
```

In a browser, this will output -

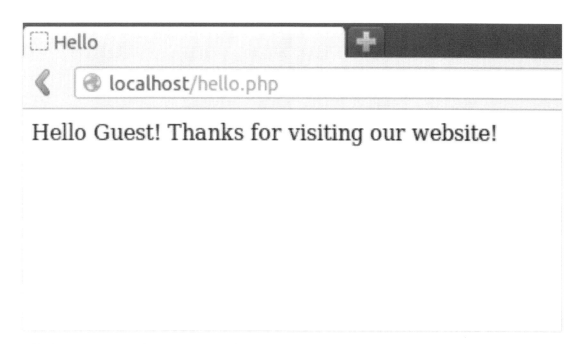

We will learn more about HTML in Chapter 3.

HTML defines the structure of web pages.

CSS

Cascading Style Sheets (CSS) specify how a HTML document will be presented to the user. With CSS, you style the different elements of HTML and also position those elements. CSS gives you complete control of the look and feel of your websites. Styles are generally defined to external style sheets, which are saved with .css extension. Your HTML files then reference those style sheets. This allows you to separate styles from actual content and gives you the opportunity to reuse the same style sheets for different HTML pages. You can learn more about CSS in Chapter 4.

CSS defines the style of web pages.

Server Side Programming Language

Server side programming languages enable us to build dynamic websites. In early days, almost all websites were static, merely a bunch of HTML documents. Those documents were just pieces of information which we couldn't do interesting stuffs like form processing, online purchases, user centric applications etc. With server side programming languages, we can do all sorts of fun stuff. The server side languages alongside databases, can give you the power to build anything you can imagine. PHP, Python, Ruby, ASP etc are some of the popular server side languages. Server side programming languages are processed in the server and the resulting HTML is sent back to the browser, so you will not be able to see the original source code of server side language from browser. In this book, you will be learning how to program such websites using PHP!

With server side programming language, we can build dynamic websites. Server side languages are processed on the server side and the resulting HTML is sent back to the client browser.

Database

Database is an essential part of modern day dynamic websites. Whether it is a forum website, a blog, an online store, you will need to store data. Though it might seem intimidating, a database is nothing more than an organized way to store data. Database enables us to retrieve or manipulate data efficiently. We create databases using DBMS (Database Management Systems) software. MySQL, Oracle, MSSQL, SQLite etc are some popular Database Management Systems. We will learn about MySQL in Chapter 11.

A database is an organized way to store data.

Overview of PHP

In the following sections, we will briefly discuss about PHP, the server side programming language we are going to learn in this book. Along the way, we will have some idea about how PHP works and also a brief overview of different versions of PHP.

What is PHP?

PHP is a server side language. PHP is currently the most popular programming language used for building dynamic websites. The best part is that newcomers will find it simple to learn. Yet, it also offers advanced features for professional programmers to build complex systems. It is fun to work with PHP and it provides you with the ability to build pretty much anything you can imagine.

PHP can be used to build all sorts of dynamic behavior to your websites. You can create web pages that interact with users through forms, build database driven websites, upload images and other files, or provide a customized experience to each user visiting your website (like what Amazon does when it shows books that you recently have browsed) and many other things.

PHP is a server side programming language. It is currently the most popular programming language for building dynamic websites.

How PHP Works?

Unlike HTML, PHP codes are interpreted and processed at server side. Let me explain a bit more. When you access an HTML file from server, the raw HTML code (the original HTML file) is sent back to the browser. Then the browser interprets the HMTL code and renders the web page. But, in case a PHP file, all the PHP codes are processed by a PHP interpreter at the server side. What it means is that, if you request a PHP file from server, the server will pass the PHP codes to the PHP interpreter and after executing the code, the server will send back the resulting HTML to the browser.

PHP codes are executed at server side and the resulting HTML codes are sent back to the browser.

A Sample PHP Script

Previously we have seen a very simple HTML file that greets the user. With PHP, in addition to show a greeting message, we can show the current date to the user as well.

```
<html>
    <head>
        <title>Hello</title>
    </head>
    <body>
        <p>Hello Guest! Thanks for visiting our website!</p>

        <p>Today's date is: <?php echo date("m/d/Y"); ?></p>
    </body>
</html>
```

Which will output -

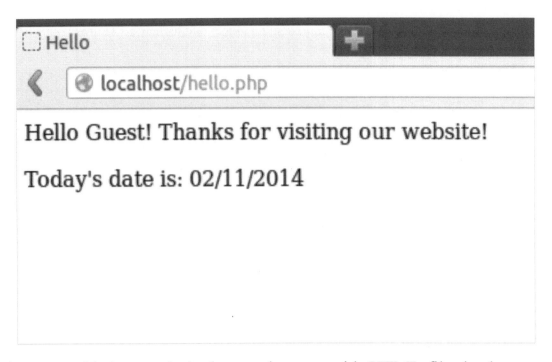

Surely we could show today's date to the user with HTML file, in that case we would do something like this -

```
<html>
      <head>
            <title>Hello</title>
      </head>
      <body>
            <p>Hello Guest! Thanks for visiting our website!</p>

            <p>Today's date is: 02/11/2014</p>
      </body>
</html>
```

It might not be obvious to you the advantage of using PHP to show date instead of HTML. But look closely at the PHP code example again. Do you see any date there? No, because we are using PHP's date function to generate the current date. So running that PHP script will always show the correct date, no matter whether you run it today or a month later. With our HTML example, we are simply hard coding the date, so the same date will be shown unless we update the date every day.

PHP date() function will give you the correct date dynamically at every moment when you call it.

10

A Brief History of PHP

Before we go on to more interesting stuff regarding PHP, let's review some history to appreciate it better. Back in 1994, Canadian software developer Rasmus Lerdorf developed a suite of CGI scripts to track visitors count for his online resume. He named the suite of scripts "Personal Home Page Tools", which was more frequently referenced as "PHP Tools". Such tools were nonexistent at that time and Lerdorf's script generated quite a bit of interest. Over time, as more functionality was desired, Rasmus rewrote the PHP Tools with new features and richer implementations and released the source to public as PHP/FI (generally referenced as PHP 2.0) on June 1995. At that point, features like database interaction, Perl-like variables, automatic interpretation of form variables, HTML embedded syntax were introduced.

Two programmers, Zeev Suraski and Andi Gutmans joined with Rasmus to collaborate in the development of a new, independent programming language. They released the updated version as PHP/FI 2 in 1997. Instead of "Personal Home Page", the acronym was changed to "PHP: HyperText Preprocessor" at that time.

By June 1998, PHP 3.0 was released. It provided mature interface for multiple databases, protocols, and API to end users. In addition, the ease of extending the language itself attracted dozens other developers who contributed with variety of modules. Object oriented programming support was also added to this new version. This is the first widely used version of PHP and more than 50,000 users were using PHP to enhance their websites.

Shortly after the official release of PHP 3.0, Andi Gutmans and Zeev Suraski had begun working on a rewrite of PHP's core. In mid-1999, they introduced "Zend Engine", the new engine to power the PHP's core. In May 2000, PHP 4.0 based on the "Zend Engine" was officially released. The new version of PHP introduced a wide range of additional features including support for more web servers, HTTP sessions, output buffering etc.

After a long developmental period, PHP 5 based on "Zend Engine 2.0" was released in July 2004. This new version contained improvements over existing features and added several features associated with mature programming languages. The object orientated capabilities were vastly improved with the introduction of PHP 5 release. Exception handling, native SQLite support, improved XML and web services support and many other improvements were also introduced.

Although it's been a while since the last official release of a major version, PHP development team is continuously working on improvements and regularly making point releases. At the time of writing this book, the latest official release was PHP 5.5.9.

PHP language originates from a suite of simple CGI scripts created by Rasmus Lerdorf in 1994. Zeev Suraski and Andi Gutmans joined with Rasmus as a core developer and they later rewrote core of PHP. PHP is now a matured programming language which supports the features of modern object orientated languages.

Summary

This chapter was an attempt to introduce you with the bigger picture of web development. Throughout the chapter, you were introduced to a wide range of technical terms. The goal wasn't to make you understand all these technologies, but instead to give you a sense of how these technologies are interconnected in the context of web development. The next chapter will take you through the steps in order to setup your development environment, so that you can start programming in PHP!

Chapter 2: Setting Up Your Development Environment

In this chapter, we will go through the steps to setup our development environment so that we can start building websites. After we setup the development environment, we will check the installation to make sure everything is working properly. We will also talk about web hosting providers, so you can deploy your website and make it accessible over the Internet. Finally, we will talk about some popular code editors which you can use to program your Php codes in.

The Development Environment

As you have learned from previous chapter, your websites will be hosted on server computers. Though you can buy all those hardware, build and maintain your own server, it is more common to buy "server space" from third party web hosting providers. You might have heard about Godday.com, Bluehost.com or Hostgator.com which are just a few of the web hosting providers, there are hundreds of such providers. They offer a wide range of packages to choose from. Once you are ready to deploy your website to public, you will definitely need to buy their services. You can also buy hosting spaces from the beginning and use that as your development environment as well. Typically, web developers tend to use their own machine as development environment and only deploy them on the web servers when they are finished. You can install the necessary software on your computer and make you're your computer run your own web server for development purpose. In this chapter, we will go through the steps needed to setup development environment on your own computer. Once you are ready to show your website to the world, you deploy it to any of web hosting service providers. The later section of this chapter will show you the steps necessary in order to publish your website.

Web developers prefer to use their own laptop/workstation as a local development environment.

Installing XAMPP

We need to install Apache web server, PHP and MySQL. We can either choose to install those independently or we can use a software package like XAMPP to install all these components at once. XAMPP is a popular PHP development environment, which contains Apache, MySQL, PHP (and Perl). XAMPP is free to install, it provides installer for all three major platforms – Windows, Mac OSX and Linux.

Follow the steps below to install XAMPP -

1. Go to the official website of XAMPP - http://www.apachefriends.org/ . You can see the installers for all three operating systems available on home page. Simply download the installer for your operating system.

2. The installation is quite straight forward, but before you start the installation, it's a good idea to check the installation instructions first. The installation instructions are available on XAMPP website. From the top level navigation menu, click "Download" and you will be directed to that page. The download page has links to documentation for all three operating systems (check right sidebar). Under the "Documentation/FAQs", click the FAQs link corresponding to your operating system.

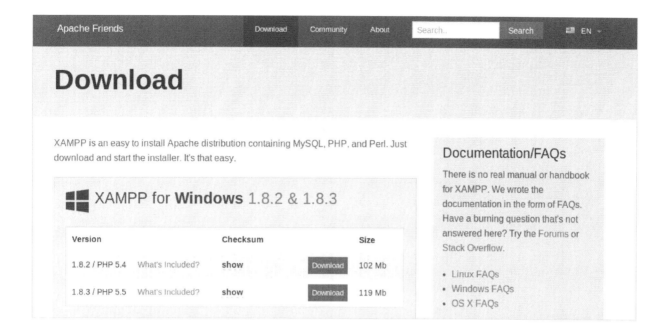

3. The FAQs page has the necessary information for installation and also other useful information for troubleshooting in case anything goes wrong.

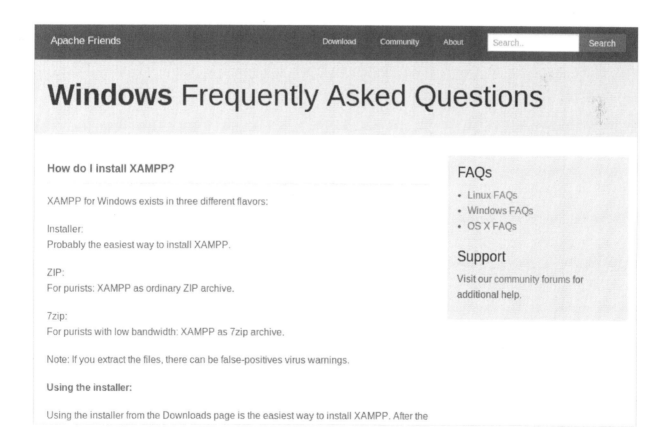

4. After you skim through the FAQs section, now run the XAMPP installer to start installation process.

For Mac OSX Users:

Open the DMG-Image file downloaded earlier and double click on the image to start installation.

For Windows Operating System Users:

Double click the exe file which you have downloaded before and then the installation process will start.

For Linux Users:

Open the terminal and navigate to the directory where you have downloaded the installer. Then change the permission of installer -

chmod 755 xampp-linux-*-installer.run

Now run the installer with the command -

sudo ./xampp-linux-*-installer.run

5. Follow the on-screen instructions to finish installation process -

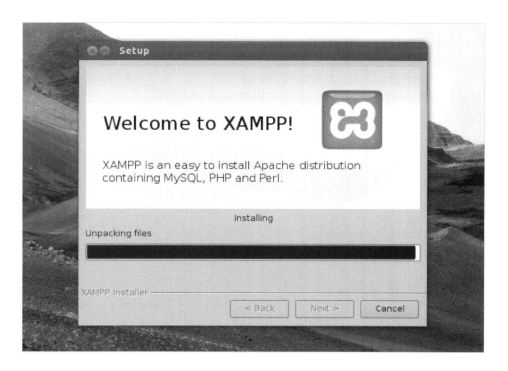

6. Default installation location of XAMPP -

For Mac OSX Users:

The default installation location of XAMPP at Mac OSX is under the directory -

/Applications/XAMPP

For Windows Operating System Users:

By default, XAMPP will be installed under the directory -

C:\xampp

For Linux Users:

Under Linux operating systems, the default installation location for XAMPP is -

/opt/lampp

XAMPP lets you setup Apache, MySQL and PHP conveniently.

Staring XAMPP

Now we have successfully installed XAMPP. Let's see how we can start XAMPP. Instructions for different operating systems are given below -

For Mac OSX Users:

To start XAMPP, you need to open XAMPP Control and then start Apache and MySQL. The name of XAMPP control is "manager-osx".

For Windows Operating System Users:

Find XAMPP control panel from Start → Programs → XAMPP and start Apache and MySQL.

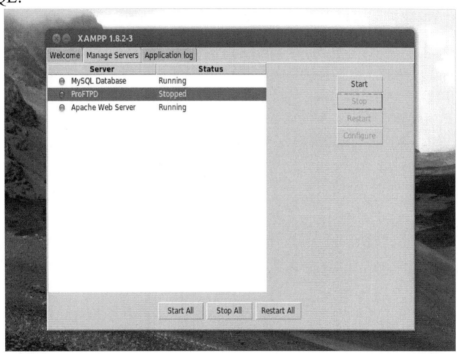

For Linux Users:

Open terminal and execute the command -

```
sudo /opt/lampp/lampp start
```

Testing Your Installation

Now we will check if the installation is successful or not. To check if the installation is successful, type the following URL at your web browser -

http://localhost/

First time you visit the URL, you will see the following splash screen -

Now choose your language and then you will see the start page of XAMPP -

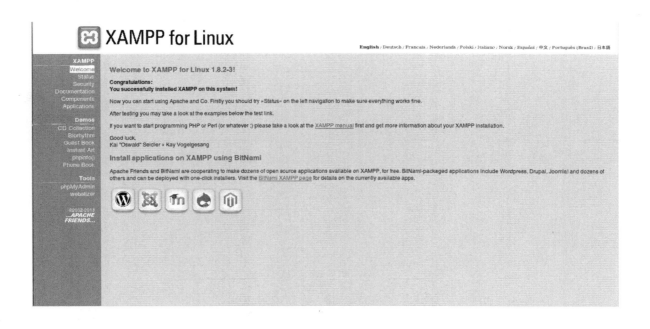

If you are getting the same results, then your XAMPP installation is working. Otherwise check the above steps again to make sure you have followed everything correctly. If you still have the problem, then revisit the FAQs section of XAMPP website mentioned earlier, that FAQs section has commonly occurred issues with solutions.

After installing XAMPP, visit http://localhost/ to make sure XAMPP is working.

Where to put Web Contents?

The 'htdocs' folder is the root directory for the web contents. You will find htdocs folder under the directory where XAMPP is installed. The default location of htdocs folder for different operating systems are specified below -

For Mac OSX Users:

The default location of htdocs folder at Mac OSX -

/Applications/XAMPP/xamppfiles/htdocs

For Windows Operating System Users:

By default, htdocs folder is located at -

C:\xampp\htdocs

For Linux Users:

Under Linux operating systems, the default location of htdocs folder is -

/opt/lampp/htdocs

You need to put your web contents under the 'htdocs' folder.

Running a Test PHP script

Now we will run a simple PHP script to get some idea how we can run our PHP programs from web server. We will run the simplest possible PHP program, which will just output a message to the browser.

```php
<?php
    echo "Hello World!";
?>
```
Save this file as hello.php and put this file under htdocs folder. Then from your browser, go to the URL -

http://localhost/hello.php

You will see the following output -

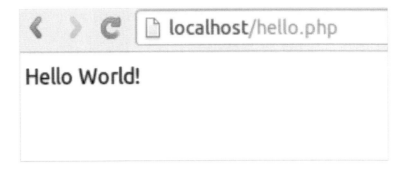

So congratulations for running your first PHP program. We are not going to understand this program right now, instead we will start exploring PHP starting from chapter 5.

Publishing Your Website

If you want to publish your website, you need two things – a domain name and a web hosting account. A domain name is the address of your website (like example.com), your visitors will enter that domain name to their browser's address bar to access your website. But you also need a server to put your website contents. You can buy both domain name and web hosting account from service providers (like godaddy.com, hostgator.com, bluehost.com, namecheap.com etc).

Once you have your domain and hosting account, then you are ready to publish your website. Now you will need to transfer contents of your website to web hosting account. Your hosting account might have graphical interface for uploading contents of your website or you can use FTP (File Transfer Protocol) software (like FileZilla, WinSCP etc) to transfer files from your own computer to your hosting account. Like htdocs folder of local sever, your hosting account will have a root directory (most commonly named public_html or www) for your web contents, you will upload files of your website under that directory. Specific instructions regarding these steps vary from provider to provider, but your hosting provider will provide step by step instructions to perform these tasks.

You will need a domain and hosting account to publish your website.

Choosing Your Code Editor

Though you can use simple text editors like Notepad for Windows or SimpleText for Mac OSX as your PHP editor, but there are some specialized editors which can make your life easier. You get syntax highlighting, code hinting, reuse code snippet etc features by using a code editor. There are hundreds of code editor out there, both commercial and open source solutions exist. I will be highlighting some popular choices, but remember to explore other editors to find your own favorite -

Notepad++

Notepad++ is a simple but elegant editor. This is available for Windows platform. It offers basic features like syntax highlighting, code hinting, matching braces, auto indentation etc. You can use this editor for free.

Sublime Text

Sublime Text is an excellent code editor. You can use this editor in all major operating systems. Though you can evaluate and test this editor for free, but a license is required for continued use.

NetBeans

NetBeans is more than a code editor, in fact this is an IDE (integrated development environment). In addition to features of regular code editors, you will get other features like code debugging, code refactoring, version control, remote connection to server etc. NetBeans will run on Windows, Mac OSX and Linux. This is also an open source project and you can use it for free. NetBeans is very popular among PHP developers.

Zend Studio

Zend Studio is by far the most powerful PHP IDE available. It is a commercial product and available to all major platforms – Windows, Mac OSX and Linux. Comprehensive code completion, version control, code debugging and refactoring, convenient code deployment and many other features are available.

Specialized code editors help you to write your programs easily by providing syntax highlighting, code suggestions, indentation and other features.

Summary

We have gone through the steps for setting up our development environment and we have checked our installation by running a simple PHP program. We have also discussed about few popular code editors, which you can use for writing PHP programs, as well as for HTML/CSS. The next chapter will introduce us with HTML, the Hyper Text Markup Language, which is used for structuring web pages.

Chapter 3: Introduction to HTML

In this chapter, we will discuss about what HTML is, how to write basic HTML documents, how to use forms, tables, lists and other elements within your HTML documents. By the end of this chapter, we will have a basic understanding of HTML. PHP programs are interpreted into HMTL pages, that's why it is important for us to have a foundational understanding of HTML.

What is HTML?

HTML stands for **H**yper **T**ext **M**arkup Language. *HTML isn't a programming language, rather it is actually a markup language.* This is the language which specifies the structure of the web pages. The HTML documents are interpreted by the browsers.

HTML documents are written in the form of HTML elements, which consist of HTML tags. HTML files are usually saved with an *.html* extension, which is recognized by the browser and then interpreted to render web pages.

A Basic HTML Document

Let's have a look at a simple HTML document first -

```
<html>
    <head>
        <title>My First HTML Page</title>
    </head>
    <body>
        <p>This is my first HTML page.</p>
    </body>
</html>
```

Before I explain the detail of how it works, first I would like to show you what it looks like when you open it with your web browser. Follow the steps below -

- Open your text editor of choice and then type the HTML code shown in the example.

- You will need to save the file with *.html* extension, don't save it with .txt or any other extension. Name it *hello.html*
- Now open the hello.html file with your favorite web browser. You can either right click the document and chose Open With option, or you can run the browser and go to browser's File → Open File option, then select the hello.html file and open it.

Once you follow the above steps, you will see something like this -

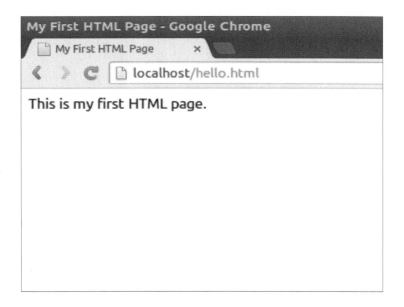

Now we will go through the example in detail and try to understand how it works -

- We can see the above HTML document starts with <html> and ends with </html>. Everything between <html> and </html> describes the web page.
- The content between <head> and </head> is the header of the HTML document, where the information about the document is placed. Within this section, we have a line of text enclosed within <title> and </title>, which defines the title of the page. When we open the HTML document with browser, we can see that *title at the browser's title bar*.
- The section within <body> and </body> is the visible page content. We have a line of text within this section, which is enclosed by <p> and </p>, which is interpreted as a paragraph.

HTML defines the structure of web pages. HTML documents are saved with a '.html' extension and are interpreted by web browsers.

HTML tags

HTML tags are keywords surrounded by angle brackets. They are the building blocks of HTML documents. The HTML tags represent the semantics or meaning, like <p> tag represents a paragraph, where <title> tag represents the title of the document. HTML tags normally come in pairs, where first tag in a pair is referred to as opening tag and second tag in known as closing tag. The closing tag is similar to the opening tag, but with a forward slash before tag name. HTML tags generally has the following form -

<tagname>Some content goes here</tagname>

For example, if we want to represent a paragraph, we use the <p> tag -

<p>This is a paragraph.</p>

HTML tags can be nested, which means a tag can be surrounded *within* another tag. In our previous example, we have already seen all other tags are nested within the <html> tag.

In the case of a nested tag, the outer tag is referred to as *parent* tag and the inner tag is referred to as a *child* tag. When using nested tags, it is important to close the child tag properly. As an example, we see that the child <title> tag is nested (opened and closed) within the <head> tag, -

```
<head>
        <title>My First HTML Page</title>
</head>
```

The following sections will discuss about commonly used tags.

HTML tags are keywords surrounded by angle brackets. They represent semantics or meanings.

The <html> tag

The <html> tag represents the beginning of an HTML document. It has the corresponding closing tag </html>, which marks the end of the document.

Everything between this pair of tags represent the web page.

The <head> tag

The <head> tag defines the header of a web page, which contains the information about the HTML document. It can have the title of the document, and also include other scripts, styles, meta informations such as – keywords, description etc.

The <title> tag

The <title> tag is a child tag of <head> tag. The <title> tag represents the title of the HTML document.

```
<title>My Web Page Title </title>
```

This title is shown in browser's title bar.

The <body> tag

The <body> tag defines the body of an HTML document. All the visible contents shown in browser window are *children* of <body> tag. It can have all sorts of contents, such as texts, images, tables, lists, forms, videos etc.

```
<body>
the contents of the document goes here...
</body>
```

Unless explicitly mentioned, all the tags discussed below will be a child of <body> tag.

Using Text Contents

You can type the plain text content directly into HTML file. But you should know that all the text formatting as well as spaces, tabs, carriage returns will be ignored by the browser. You need to use corresponding HTML tags to explicitly set the text formatting. Take a look at an example -

```
This is a a text content
    with formatting,
```

which will be   ignored by the browser.

If we put this text into an HTML file, we will get following output -

This is a a text content with formatting, which will be ignored by the browser.

Within HTML documents, you can use plain text contents directly.

Text Formatting

You can use different HTML tags to format text, like make them bold or italic. Let's see some examples with corresponding output -

Boldface

We use the <b> tag to format the text as bold -

<b>This content is formatted to boldface.<b>

This will output:

This content is formatted to boldface.

Italic

The <i> tag can be used to make the text italic -

This content will be formatted to italic.

This will output -

This content will be formatted to italic.

Both Boldface and Italic

This example shows how we can nest <i> tag within <b> tag -

```
<b><i>This is both boldface and italic</i></b>
```

Which will output -

This is both boldface & italic

Though you can use HTML tags for text formatting, we will typically use CSS for formatting purposes. CSS is covered in the next chapter.

Using Line Breaks

You can use <br/> tag to explicitly tell the browser to insert a line break. Previously we have seen HTML tags come in pairs, but <br/> tag has no closing tag. When the browser will encounter a <br/> tag, it will insert a line break.

```
This is first line.<br/>This is second line.
<br/>
Yet another line.
```

This will output -

```
This is first line.
This is second line.
Yet another line.
```

Use the <br/> tag to insert a line break.

Defining Paragraphs

The <p> tag is used to define paragraphs. Let's see an example of using <p> tag -

```
<p>This is a paragraph.</p>
<p>This is another paragraph.</p>
```

You will see that, browser automatically adds some spacing before and after the

<p> tag.

> This is a paragraph.
>
> This is another paragraph.

The Heading Tags

You can use heading tags to create titles. There are six heading tags available to create titles of different sizes, where <h1> will create largest title and <h6> will create smallest title -

```
<h1>This is a heading</h1>
<h2>This is a heading</h2>
<h3>This is a heading</h3>
<h4>This is a heading</h4>
<h5>This is a heading</h5>
<h6>This is a heading</h6>
```

The above will have the following output –

This is a heading

This is a heading

This is a heading

This is a heading

This is a heading

This is a heading

Similar to paragraph tag, heading tags also leave some space before and after the tag.

Creating Lists

You can create both ordered and unordered list using HTML. Ordered lists are defined using <ol> and unordered lists are defined using <ul> tag. The list items of both ordered and unordered lists are defined using <li> tag.

Lets create an ordered list first -

```
<ol>
      <li>Item 1</li>
      <li>Item 2</li>
      <li>Item 3</li>
      <li>Item 4</li>
      <li>Item 5</li>
</ol>
```

We will have the following output -

```
1. Item 1
2. Item 2
3. Item 3
4. Item 4
5. Item 5
```

Now let's see how we can create an unordered list -

```
<ul>
      <li>Item 1</li>
      <li>Item 2</li>
      <li>Item 3</li>
      <li>Item 4</li>
      <li>Item 5</li>
</ul>
```

This will output -

- Item 1
- Item 2
- Item 3
- Item 4
- Item 5

With HTML, you can create both ordered and unordered lists.

Creating Tables

The <table> tag can be used to define a HTML table. The rows of the able are defined using the <tr> tag and we use <td> tag to represent a column within a row. Let's see an example -

```
<table border="1">
    <tr>
        <td>Serial</td>
        <td>Name</td>
    </tr>
    <tr>
        <td>1001</td>
        <td>J. Smith</td>
    </tr>
    <tr>
        <td>1002</td>
        <td>R. Stuart</td>
    </tr>

    <tr>
        <td>1003</td>
        <td>Andrew Russel</td>
    </tr>
</table>
```

This will output -

Serial	Name
1001	J. Smith
1002	R. Stuart
1003	Andrew Russel

Notice the opening table tag (<table border="1">). We have provided an additional information here, the border width. This is known as an *attribute*. We use attributes in a tag in order to provide additional information.

The HTML <table> tag can be used to represent data in a tabular form.

Adding Images

The <img> tag is used to add images to your web pages. You specify the image file path using the *src* attribute of <img> tag. Take a look at example below -

<img src="moon.jpg" />

Save the above line of code as *picture.html* and put an image named "moon.jpg" within the same directory where we put the HTML file (picture.html). Running the HTML file should display the image -

If you put the image within a sub-directory (say within images directory) under the directory where the HTML file is stored, then you can refer to the image file source like this -

```
<img src="images/moon.jpg"/>
```

You can use width and height attributes to control the width and height of the image resource -

```
<img src="mypic.jpg" width="200px" height="200px"/>
```

With the '<img>' tag, you can insert images in your HTML pages.

Creating Hyperlinks

You can use anchor tag (<a>) to create hyperlinks. The **href** attribute of anchor tag is used to provide the *url* of the target website (or web page). Let's see an example -

```
<a href="http://www.google.com">Click here</a> to visit google's website.
```

You will see the following output if you run the above example -

Click here to visit google's website.

Notice the text "Click here" is underlined with blue color, we provide that text between <a> and </a>. This text will be treated as hyperlink and you can click that to navigate to new page. Within href attribute, you can also provide link of your another page as well -

The <a href="contact.html">contact page</a> of the website contains detailed information on how to contact with me.

Instead of text within <a> and </a>, you can also use image file to make that image a click-able link -

```
<a href="about.html"><img src="image.jpg"/></a>
```

Hyperlinks are created using the anchor tag (<a>).

HTML Forms

HTML forms are the main way of interaction between users and your website. You can collect your user's valuable comments and feedback via forms. Contact forms allow your users to send mail from within your website. Registration and login forms enable you to create user centric websites. These are just some of the many examples of using forms. Thus, it is very important to have a good understanding of HTML forms. You will later see how we can access form data using PHP programming language.

The <form> tag is used to create an HTML form. Let's have a look at a basic HTML form -

```
<form>
input elements...
</form>
```

An HTML form can have different type of input elements, like – text fields, check-boxes, radio buttons, drop-down lists etc.

HTML forms are used to interact with your website users.

Adding Text Fields

The text fields are the most common input elements of forms, you can add any text field with <input> tag and specifying the **"type"** attribute as "text".

Let's see how we can add text fields to our form -

```
<form>
Name: <input type="text" name="name"/><br/>
Email: <input type="text" name="email"/>
</form>
```

This will give following output -

Name: [   ]
Email: [   ]

The name attribute of <input> tag is usually used by PHP to access the input data from within PHP code.

Text input fields can take in all sorts of text values, for e.g. – name, address, email or any other pieces of textual information.

Using Password Fields

A Password field is similar to text fields, but the characters are masked (usually the characters are shown as circles or stars). The <input> tag with **"type"** attribute set to "password" can be used as password input field -
<form>
Password: <input type="password" name="password"/>
</form>

The below screen shot shows the password input box with sample input -

Password: ●●●●●●●●●|

Within password input fields, the characters are masked.

Radio Buttons

If you want to let the user select only an item from a set of options, radio buttons are a good choice. Using <input> tag with **"type"** attribute set to "radio" can be used to create radio buttons -

<form>
Select your gender
<input type="radio" name="sex" value="male"/> Male
<input type="radio" name="sex" value="female"/>Female
</form>

You will see the following output -

Select your gender
○ Male
○ Female

Important! Note that you should give the same **name** attribute to all the options for that particular choice. You can set the value of the options using the **value** attribute.

Radio buttons are appropriate when you want to give users options to choose from among alternatives.

Check-boxes

Check-boxes let the user chose zero or more options from a set of options. <input> tag with attribute **"type"** set to "checkbox" is used to define checkboxes -

```
<form>
Select The Programming Lanauges You Know<br/>
<input type="checkbox" name="language" value="PHP"/>PHP<br/>
<input type="checkbox" name="language" value="Python"/>Python<br/>
<input type="checkbox" name="language" value="Java"/>Java<br/>
<input type="checkbox" name="language" value="Ruby"/>Ruby
</form>
```

This will output -

Select The Programming Lanauges You Know
☐ PHP
☐ Python
☐ Java
☐ Ruby

With check-boxes, users can choose multiple options.

Drop-down Lists

The <select> tag is used to create the drop-down list, while the <option> tag is used to add options to your drop-down list.

```
<form>
Which of the following browser you use?<br/>
<select name="browser">
      <option value="chrome">Google Chrome</option>
      <option value="firefox">Firefox</option>
      <option value="safari">Safari</option>
      <option value="ie">Internet Explorer</option>
</select>
</form>
```

You can see that a drop-down list is created. If you click the little arrow, other options will be revealed -

With <select> tag, you can create drop-down lists.

Textarea

Sometimes you need a large text input area, say you want to post an article to your blog. <textarea> tag is used to create large multi-line text input boxes -

```
<form>
Enter your article-<br/>
<textarea name="article" rows="10" cols="50">
</textarea>
</form>
```
The above will output this -

Enter your article-

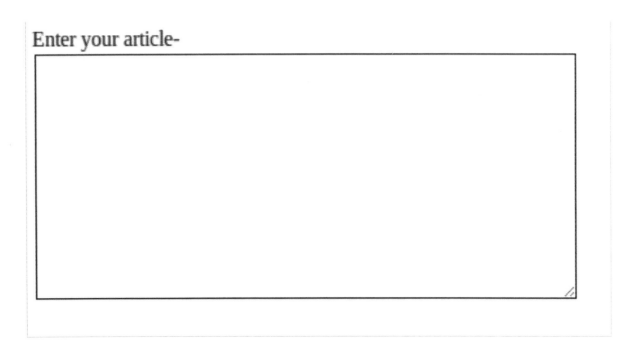

The *rows* and *cols* attributes are used to set the row and column dimensions respectively.

Textareas are appropriate for accepting a large block of text from users.

Adding a Submit Button

So far we have discussed different input elements of HTML. But an important piece is still missing, the *submit* button. You can use the <input> tag with **"type"** attribute set to "submit" -

<input type="submit" value="Submit"/>

This will output a submit button -

Submit

With **"value"** attribute, you can set the label of submit button.

How it all fits together - A Sample Signup Form

Finally, we will see how different input elements fit together to create a simple user signup form -

```html
<form>

    <table>
        <tr>
            <td>First Name</td>
            <td><input type="text" name="firstname"/></td>
        </tr>
        <tr>

            <td>Last Name</td>
            <td><input type="text" name="lastname"/></td>
        </tr>
        <tr>

            <td>Username</td>
            <td><input type="text" name="username"/></td>
        </tr>
        <tr>

            <td>Password</td>
            <td><input type="password" name="password"/></td>
        </tr>
        <tr>

            <td>Email</td>
            <td><input type="text" name="email"/></td>
        </tr>
        <tr>

            <td>Gender</td>
            <td>

                <input type="radio" name="sex" value="male"/>Male
                <input type="radio" name="sex"
value="female">Female
            </td>
        </tr>
        <tr>

            <td>andnbsp;</td>
            <td><input type="submit" name="submit" value="Signup"/></
td>
        </tr>
    </table>

</form>
```

The above form will look something like this -

First Name	
Last Name	
Username	
Password	
Email	
Gender	○ Male ○ Female
	[Signup]

Later we will see how we can use PHP to process the form. We will be doing that in a later chapter.

Inspecting the HTML code from Browser

In our first chapter, I have mentioned that the HTML codes are interpreted by the browsers. Which means if your web browser requests an HTML file from web server, the web server will send the HTML code to the browser. Then it is the job of your web browser to interpret that HTML code and display it. That's why you will be able to see the HTML code from the browser.

Use the **View Page Source** option to view the original HTML code. From your browser window, right click and you will see an option **View Page Source** or you can use the browser's menu option **Tools** → **View Source**.

Let's run our above registration form to our web browser and we will see the source code from browser -

```
<form>

    <table>
        <tr>
            <td>First Name</td>
            <td><input type="text" name="firstname"/></td>
        </tr>
        <tr>
            <td>Last Name</td>
            <td><input type="text" name="lastname"/></td>
        </tr>
        <tr>
            <td>Username</td>
            <td><input type="text" name="username"/></td>
        </tr>
        <tr>
            <td>Password</td>
            <td><input type="password" name="password"/></td>
        </tr>
        <tr>
            <td>Email</td>
            <td><input type="text" name="email"/></td>
        </tr>
        <tr>
            <td>Gender</td>
            <td>
                <input type="radio" name="sex" value="male"/>Male
                <input type="radio" name="sex" value="female">Female
            </td>
        </tr>
        <tr>
            <td> </td>
            <td><input type="submit" name="submit" value="Signup"/></td>
        </tr>
    </table>

</form>
```

HTML codes are interpreted by web browsers and that's why we can see the HTML code from a browser.

Summary

This chapter introduces you with HTML, which defines the structure of the web pages. We have learned the basics of HTML in this chapter, next chapter will introduce us with Cascading Style Sheet (CSS), a language used for styling the web pages.

Chapter 4: Styling Web Pages with CSS

The previous chapter introduced us to HTML, a markup language to specify the structure of web pages. In this chapter, we will learn how we can style the web pages with Cascading Style Sheets (CSS). You can think of HTML as the meaning or content, where CSS defines the presentation or appearance of your document.

What is CSS?

CSS stands for **C**ascading **S**tyle **S**heets. You can think of CSS as a language which specify how the HTML documents are presented to the users. In the previous chapter, you have learned how to create HTML documents with different elements. You have created paragraphs, tables, lists, forms etc. With CSS, you can style those elements, adjust the size, font-family, color of texts, add background images, style buttons, lists, table, forms etc. You can set where different elements will be placed in your web pages. Essentially, you can style your web pages to look and feel the way you desire.

CSS is the language which specifies how HTML documents will be presented to users.

Your First CSS File

In this section, we will see how to create a very simple CSS file and link that CSS file with an HTML document. First let's create a simple HTML document -

```
<html>
    <head>
        <title>My Web Page</title>
    </head>
    <body>
        <p>This is a paragraph.</p>
    </body>
</html>
```

Save this file as *webpage.html* and run it from the browser. You will see the following output with a single paragraph -

This is a paragraph.

Now we will see how we can write a very simple CSS file to style the paragraph of the HTML document. Instead of the default black color, we will change the color of the paragraph text to red. The following CSS code will do that -

```
p {
    color: red;
}
```

Create a new file with the above CSS code, save the file as *style.css* and put this file under the same directory where we stored our webpage.html file. I will explain the CSS syntax later, first we will see how it looks in the browser.

If we run the webpage.html again, we will see the HTML file looks exactly like previous one -

This is a paragraph.

Though we have created the CSS file, but we haven't told our HTML file to use that file CSS file yet. Now let's see tell our HTML file to use that CSS file. We use <link> tag to link a CSS file from within our HTML file -

```
<html>
    <head>
        <title>My Web Page</title>

        <link rel="stylesheet" type="text/css" href="style.css" />
    </head>
    <body>
        <p>This is a paragraph.</p>
    </body>
</html>
```

Notice the <link> tag (the bold line). Now we need to save the webpage.html file and if we run the webpage.html file again (or just refresh from browser), we will see following output -

This is a paragraph.

Now we can see the style is applied to our HTML file, as a result the color of the paragraph text is changed to red.

The HTML <link> tag is used to link an external CSS file from within a HTML file.

Putting CSS within your HTML File

The previous section shows us how to create an external CSS file and link that CSS file from with HTML file. This is what developers typically do in using external CSS files to store style elements. But you can also place the CSS code inside the HTML file as well. This is done using the <style> tag, which is typically placed within the HTML <head> tag. We can rewrite the previous example as follows -

```
<html>
     <head>
          <title>My Web Page</title>

          <style>
               p {
                    color: red;
               }
          </style>
     </head>
     <body>
          <p>This is a paragraph.</p>
     </body>
</html>
```

If we save this HTML file and run it from the browser, we will see the paragraph text colored to red as well -

This is a paragraph.

You might be wondering, if CSS files can be placed inside a HTML file, why should we go through the trouble of creating external CSS files? Well, putting CSS in an external file has several benefits. First, separating HTML and CSS within distinct files gives us separation between structure of the documents (which is defined by the HTML file) and the style (which is defined within the CSS file). By creating an external CSS file, we can apply the same style sheet to multiple HTML files. Also if we need to update the styles, we don't have to go through each individual HTML files. We can just edit the CSS files straight for the change to apply to all the HTML files.

Using external CSS files enable us to reuse the same style for multiple web pages.

CSS Syntax Explained

The basic syntax of CSS is as follows -

```
selector {
        property: value;
}
```

So we can see there are three parts here, first one is called the **selector**, which is followed by curly braces. Within the curly braces, you will find pair of **property** and **value** separated by colon (:). Finally the line ends with a semicolon (;). The above syntax is referred as a CSS **rule set**.

The CSS **selector** determines which HTML elements will be stylized. For different HTML tags, you can use the tag names as CSS selectors. For example - <p>, <h1>, <a> etc. can be targeted by the corresponding selectors **p**, **h1** and **a**.

Now let's talk about the **property** part of the rule set. Each HTML element will have some properties. For example, the image element will have width and height properties. Once you target an element with **selector**, then you can apply styles to those elements by setting **value** of different **property** of that element. Each

47

property-value pair is separated by a color (:), you will end the property-value pair with semicolon (;). You can put multiple property-value pairs within the curly braces. Let's take a look at another example of applying style to a paragraph element. (Note that for learning purposes and to make things simple, we are putting CSS rules within HTML file)

```html
<html>
    <head>
        <title>CSS Demo</title>

        <style>
            p {
                font-size: 20px;
                color: red;
                text-decoration: underline;
            }
        </style>
    </head>
    <body>
        <p>This is a paragraph.</p>
    </body>
</html>
```

Save the above code within an HTML file and run it in the browser. You will see the following output -

<u>This is a paragraph.</u>

If you look at the CSS rules of the above example, you will see that we have targeted the paragraph using the selector "p". Within the curly braces, we have set values for three properties. We set font size to 20px, text color to red and also underlined the text.

You can use HTML tag names as a selector name to target HTML elements. These elements can be stylized by setting the values of different properties.

Using Multiple Selectors

We can use multiple selectors separating them with comma (,). Let's see how we can target both heading and paragraph -

```
<html>
    <head>
        <title>CSS Demo</title>

        <style>
            p, h1 {
                color: red;
                font-family: Arial;
            }
        </style>
    </head>
    <body>
        <h1>Welcome</h1>
        <p>Welcome to our website!</p>
    </body>
</html>
```

This will output -

Welcome

Welcome to our website!

Here we have used both *p* and *h1* as selectors, that's why the style is applied to both elements.

You can use multiple selectors to apply the same styles to multiple elements.

ID Selectors

You can define an ID selector using a hash sign (#) followed by a string of characters. This selector will match any HTML element which has an ID attribute of same value (without # sign). Let's have a look at the following example -

```
<html>
    <head>
        <title>CSS Demo</title>

        <style>
            #emphasis {
                color: red;
            }
        </style>
    </head>
    <body>
        <p id="emphasis">This is a paragraph.</p>
        <p>This is another paragraph.</p>
    </body>
</html>
```

If we run this example, we will have following output -

This is a paragraph.

This is another paragraph.

We can see that our HTML file has two paragraphs, the first paragraph has an ID attribute of value "emphasis". Within our CSS rule set, we have used the ID selector to target that paragraph -

```
#emphasis {
    ...
}
```

Here, any HTML element with ID attribute of "emphasis" will be stylized. One thing you need to remember, within any HTML page, there should be a single HTML element of a given ID. So in our previous example, there should be only a single HTML element with ID of "emphasis".

A string of characters preceded by a hash sign (#) defines an ID selector which will select any HTML element of that ID attribute. There should be only one instance of a given ID within any HTML page.

Class Selectors

Class selectors are similar to ID selectors, but unlike hash sign (#), in the case of class selectors, the character string is preceded by a period sign (.). Any HTML element with class attribute of the same value (without period sign) will be matched. In the case of a class attribute within a HTML file, you can use the same class to as many elements as you need. Let's have a look at an example -

```
<html>
    <head>
        <title>CSS Demo</title>

        <style>
            .emphasis {
                color: red;
            }
        </style>
    </head>
    <body>
        <h1 class="emphasis">Sample Heading</h1>
        <p>This is a paragraph.</p>
        <p  class="emphasis">This is another paragraph.</p>
    </body>
</html>
```

This will output -

Sample Heading

This is a paragraph.

This is another paragraph.

Here we have used the same class to the heading and the second paragraph. That's why our class selector matches both elements and apply styles to them.

You can use the same class value for multiple elements within a HTML page.

Combining Selectors and Style Inheritance

The beauty of CSS is the ability to combine selectors and inherit styles, which enables us to define generic styles to elements and then we can define more specific styles as necessary. Let's have a look at this concept of inheritance of style -

```html
<html>
    <head>
        <title>CSS Demo</title>

        <style>
            h1, p {
                font-family: Sans;
            }

            h1 {
                font-size: 22px;
            }

            p {
                font-size: 14px;
            }

            p.emphasis {
                color: red;
            }
        </style>
    </head>
    <body>
        <h1 class="emphasis">Sample Heading</h1>
        <p>This is a paragraph.</p>
        <p class="emphasis">This is another paragraph.</p>
```

```
        </body>
</html>
```

This will output -

Sample Heading

This is a paragraph.

This is another paragraph.

Let's have a closer look at the CSS rule set of the above example. We first set font-family of all text elements. This will apply style to two paragraphs and one heading -

```
h1, p {
        font-family: Sans;
}
```

Then set font size of heading -

```
h1 {
        font-size: 22px;
}
```

<h1> element will inherit font-family from previous rule and also will have font-size specified.

Similarly, when we set font-size of paragraphs, it will also inherit font-family as well.

Finally we have combined selectors to select paragraph with class attribute of "emphasis" to make the text color red -

```
p.emphasis {
        color: red;
}
```

Though we have two elements with class "emphasis" (one heading and one paragraph), we have combined element selector with class selector to further narrow down the selection to only paragraph element with class attribute of "emphasis". This paragraph will inherit both font-family and font-size properties. We could also overwrite any of the inherited properties with new property -

```
p.emphasis {
     color: red;
     font-size: 18px;
}
```

In this case, font-size property of paragraph with class "emphasis" will overwrite the previous font-size set by more generic rule -

```
p {
     font-size: 14px;
}
```

You can define generic styles to common elements and then apply specific styles as necessary.

The HTML <div> Tag

HTML <div> tag plays an important role for defining layout with CSS. Using <div> tag, we can define a division or a section in an HTML document. This <div> tag is usually used to group HTML elements so that they can be formatted using CSS. Let's use a <div> tag to group a heading and a paragraph element -

```
<div>
     <h1>This is a heading.</h1>
     <p>This is a paragraphs.</p>
</div>
```

You can select a <div> as follows -

```
div {
     ...
}
```

The <div> tag can have class or ID attributes as well.

54

```
<div class="content">
        ...
</div>
```

Then you can select this as follows -

```
div.content {
        ...
}
```

With <div> tag, you can create sections in your HTML document to hold different elements.

Block Level Elements

When dealing with CSS, you might come across the term "block level element". Block level elements are those elements that are formatted visually as blocks. Elements like <div> , <p>, <h1>, <h2> are some examples of block level elements.

Block level elements are more structural, layout related elements. If the width of a block level element isn't specified, it will expand horizontally to fit inside its parent container and will also expand vertically to hold its contents.

Let's see how we can set the width and height of a paragraph -

```
<html>
<head>
        <title>CSS Demo</title>

        <style>
                p{
                        width: 600px;
                        height: 200px;
                        border: 1px solid #000000;
                }
        </style>
</head>
<body>
        <p>
                Lorem Ipsum is simply dummy text of the printing and typesetting
```

```
                  industry. Lorem Ipsum has been the industry's standard dummy
text ever         since the 1500s, when an unknown printer took a galley of type
and               scrambled it to make a type specimen book. It has survived not
only five         centuries, but also the leap into electronic typesetting,
remaining               essentially unchanged.
        </p>
</body>
</html>
```

This will output -

```
Lorem Ipsum is simply dummy text of the printing and typesetting industry. Lorem
Ipsum has been the industry's standard dummy text ever since the 1500s, when an
unknown printer took a galley of type and scrambled it to make a type specimen
book. It has survived not only five centuries, but also the leap into electronic
typesetting, remaining essentially unchanged.
```

We have also specified a border around the paragraph by specifying three values -
- 1px – which tells the border will be 1 pixel width
- solid – defines border outline as solid
- #000000 – specifies border color as black, this is hexadecimal code for black color

Applying Padding

Padding is the space around the content. In our previous example, we can see the border of the paragraph is very close to the paragraph texts. We can apply padding to the paragraph texts by setting values for padding property. You can specify padding for an individual side (like padding-left: 10px) or for all sides at once (like padding: 10px 20px 15px 25px). If you want to apply uniform padding to all sides, you can use just one value for padding property (like padding: 10px). Let's see how we can apply padding to our previous example -

```
<html>
<head>
        <title>CSS Demo</title>

        <style>
                p{
                        width: 600px;
```

```
                height: 200px;
                border: 1px solid #000000;
                padding: 20px;
            }
    </style>
</head>
<body>
    <p>
            Lorem Ipsum is simply dummy text of the printing and typesetting
            industry. Lorem Ipsum has been the industry's standard dummy
text ever           since the 1500s, when an unknown printer took a galley of type
and                 scrambled it to make a type specimen book. It has survived not
only five           centuries, but also the leap into electronic typesetting,
remaining              essentially unchanged.
    </p>
</body>
</html>
```

This will set a padding of 20px to all sides -

Lorem Ipsum is simply dummy text of the printing and typesetting industry. Lorem Ipsum has been the industry's standard dummy text ever since the 1500s, when an unknown printer took a galley of type and scrambled it to make a type specimen book. It has survived not only five centuries, but also the leap into electronic typesetting, remaining essentially unchanged.

With the padding property, we can leave space around the content of an element.

Applying Margin

With margin property, you can set a space between your targeted element and its surroundings. The syntax for defining margin is similar to padding (like margin: 20px or margin-left: 30px etc). Let's add margin to our previous example -

```
<html>
<head>
    <title>CSS Demo</title>
```

```
<style>
    p{
        width: 600px;
        height: 200px;
        border: 1px solid #000000;
        padding: 20px;
        margin-left: 100px;
    }
</style>
</head>
<body>
    <p>
        Lorem Ipsum is simply dummy text of the printing and typesetting
        industry. Lorem Ipsum has been the industry's standard dummy
text ever       since the 1500s, when an unknown printer took a galley of type
and             scrambled it to make a type specimen book. It has survived not
only five        centuries, but also the leap into electronic typesetting,
remaining               essentially unchanged.
    </p>
</body>
</html>
```

Let's see how it looks after applying 100px margin to left -

> Lorem Ipsum is simply dummy text of the printing and typesetting industry. Lorem Ipsum has been the industry's standard dummy text ever since the 1500s, when an unknown printer took a galley of type and scrambled it to make a type specimen book. It has survived not only five centuries, but also the leap into electronic typesetting, remaining essentially unchanged.

With the margin property, we can set space between the targeted element and it's surroundings.

Further Reading

We have learned the basics of CSS so far. Along the way, you have seen a few of the properties of some common HTML elements. There are many other properties available which we can't cover all of them. But you can easily learn about those by consulting online materials, there are tons of excellent free online resources available. W3Schools.com is one of them. Check out the CSS section of w3schools here - http://www.w3schools.com/css/default.asp .

Summary

This chapter introduced us to CSS, the language to style our web pages. From the next chapter on, we will begin learning PHP, the server side programming language to build dynamic websites. The next chapter will be an introduction to PHP, covering foundational programming concepts. If you don't have any prior programming experience or are just a beginner, don't worry, we will start from the basics.
experience. We will start from very basics.

Chapter 5: Introducing PHP

In this chapter we are going to begin exploring the exciting world of PHPH programming. We will start from the foundational basics, so don't worry if you haven't started or is just a beginner at programming. Soon, you will start writing programs that can do interesting stuffs. In this chapter, you will learn how to write your very first PHP program. You will be familiar with how to embed PHP code into your HTML pages. You will also learn how to output data to the browser and finally the concept of *comments* in PHP.

A simple "Hello World" program

We begin by writing our first PHP program. We will write a simple program which outputs "Hello World" to the browser. This is referred to as the "Hello World" program which is typically used to as an introduction to any programming language. Follow these simple steps -

- Create a new file and save as *hello.php*, notice the file extension here. Do not use .html or .txt or any other extension, instead save it with .php extension.
- Put the following code block and save it.

```php
<?php
        echo "Hello World";
?>
```

- Save this file under the root directory of your web server (it is *htdocs* folder, don't you remember?)
- Open your favorite web browser and enter the address http://localhost/hello.php to your web browser's address bar and press enter.
- If everything goes fine, you should see something like this -

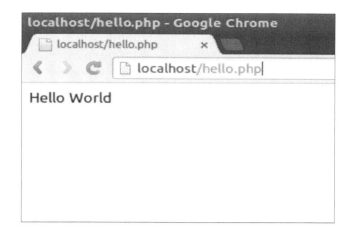

If you get something different, then most probably your web server and PHP installation wasn't done correctly. Revisit the installation instructions and make sure you perform each step carefully.

You need to put your PHP files under web server (the htdocs folder). PHP files are saved with .php extension.

Hello World Program Explained

Now let's step through the "Hello World" program we have written and try to understand how it is working -

Line 1

```php
<?php
```

"**<?php**" is the opening PHP tag, which indicates the beginning of a PHP code block. Anything written after that tag will be considered as PHP code.

Line 2

```php
echo "Hello World";
```

"**echo**" is a language construct that outputs a *string* (we will discuss more about string later. For now, *string* basically refers to a sequence of characters). So in this line, we output the string "Hello World" to the browser.

Notice the semicolon (**;**) at the end of the line. The semicolon at the end of the line indicates the end of the *statement* (*statement* is just an alternative name for a command or instruction. We give instructions to the computer one by one and then use semicolon to indicate the end of that instruction).

Line 3

```
    ?>
```

"**?>**" is the closing PHP tag, which tells that, our PHP code block ends here and everything following this line isn't PHP code.

PHP codes are enclosed within a opening PHP tag (<?php) and closing PHP tag (?>).

Embedding PHP code into your HTML pages

In our simple "Hello World" program, we have seen how to output a string to the browser. Now we will see how we can embed a PHP code block into a HTML page. But one thing you must remember, since you are going to use PHP code into your HTML page, your HTML page must be saved with .php extension instead of .html extension. Otherwise, the web server will not recognize this as PHP file. Let's see the below example -

```
<html>
    <head>
        <title>My First Web Page</title>
    </head>
    <body>
        <h3>My First Web Page</h3>

        <?php
            echo "This is my first PHP Enabled Web Page";
        ?>
    </body>
</html>
```

Seems familiar, right? Actually you already know everything you need to put a

PHP code block into your HTML page. You just insert a PHP code block starting with opening PHP tag **(<?php)** and ending with closing PHP tag **(?>)**.

Now let's run the above example. If you don't remember how to do this, then just follow these steps -

- Create a new file with the above code and save as *webpage.php*
- Put this file under the root directory of your web server (*htdocs* folder).
- Open your web browser and enter the address http://localhost/webpage.php to your web browser's address bar and press enter.
- Now you should see something like this -

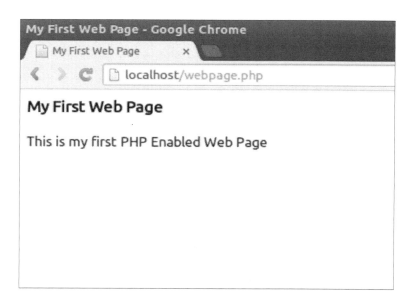

Few points to note...

- Whenever you want to use PHP code into your HTML page, remember not to save that file with .html extension, instead you should save that file with .php extension.
- You can insert a PHP code block anywhere into your HTML pages (but they must be enclosed within PHP tag).
- You can put as many PHP code block into a single HTML page as you like. But don't put unnecessary code blocks, only use as many code blocks you need.

If you want to use PHP code in a HTML page, you must save the file with .php extension and enclose the PHP code block within PHP tags.

Outputting data to the browser

We have seen how to output data to the browser in the two preceding examples using **echo**. But I want to mention another similar function which you will often come across. The **print** function does a similar job to **echo**. You can use **print** instead of **echo** to output string.

```php
<?php
    print "Hello World";
?>
```

This will also output "Hello World" to the browser.

You might see another version of both **echo** and **print**, they can be used with parenthesis -

```php
<?php
    print("Hello World");
    echo("Hello World");
?>
```

You can use any version you like, whether with or without parenthesis. It's just a good practise to be consistent throughout your code.

A few words regarding whether you should use **echo** or **print**. Both **echo** and **print** does the same job, using one over other is not likely to yield performance improvements. (the difference between these two is irrelevant to you, but in case you are curious, **print** always returns 1, but **echo** returns nothing. We will talk about return value later, when we discuss about functions.)

You can use either the print() or echo() function to output data to the browser.

Output HTML with PHP

You can also output any HTML code block using PHP. All you need to do is to

64

wrap the HTML code within quotes and make that a PHP string. Let's see an example -

```php
<?php
    echo "<strong>Hello World</strong>";
?>
```

Here we have used "**<strong>**" tag to make the text "Hello World" bold. If you save this code and run, then you will see that the output is in bold text -

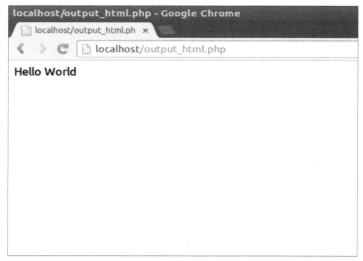

In fact you can output any HTML code, including table, list etc -

```php
<?php
    echo "<ul>
            <li>Item 1</li>
            <li>Item 2</li>
            <li>Item 3</li>
        </ul>";
?>
```

Which will output something like this -

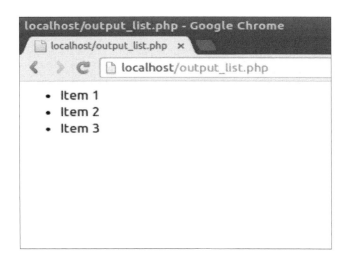

You can see that we output a list with **echo**. This is just for demonstration that you can output list with PHP. The general rule however, it is best to avoid outputting HTML with PHP. Use HTML code block to output standard HTML elements and then use PHP code to output dynamic content only.

You can output HTML code using PHP.

PHP source codes are not shown in

Remember that we can view the HTML and CSS source code from browser (if you can't recall, it's view source option from browser). Now you might be interested in doing the same thing with PHP code. But you will not be able to view source code for PHP from the browser's view source option. As we have said earlier, PHP is processed on the server side and the resulting HTML code is sent back to the browser.

PHP codes are processed on server side and resulting HTML codes are returned to browser. You will be able to view HTML code from browser.

Using Comments in PHP

Although we have some written simple programs, we will progress through the rest of the book and learn about other language features, programming techniques to write more complex programs. Once the complexity of the program grows, you will be using more in-depth logic to accomplish certain tasks. When someone else looks at your code, he might not be able to understand what your logic was by simply looking through your code. Or consider yourself making modifications or enhancements to the program written a few months or even years ago. During then, everything will not be as intuitive even though that code was written by yourself. That's why programmers use comments to make notes within codes. In PHP, you can make a single line comment by starting the line with double slash characters (//).

```php
<?php
    //this is a single line comment
?>
```

Comments are ignored by PHP interpreter. They are meant to for the sole purpose of being read and understood by human. Sometimes, you may need to make multi-line comments. You can do that by beginning with the character sequence "/*" and ending with "*/". Let's have a look at the example -

```php
<?php
    /* This is the first line of a multi-line comment.
       This is the second line. */
?>
```

When you make comments in your code, remember to use it intelligently. Comments are particularly useful when you are doing something that isn't so obvious from the code.

Use comments to make notes for yourself or other programmers.

Example: Displaying Day of the Week and Current Date

Now let's see an example of a PHP script which will greet the user and display the day of the week and current date -

```
<html>
    <head>
        <title>My Web Page</title>
    </head>
    <body>
        <h2>Welcome Guest!</h2>
```

```
            <p>Today is <?php echo date("l"); ?></p>
            <p>Current date is: <?php echo date("m/d/Y"); ?></p>
        </body>
</html>
```

This will output -

Welcome Guest!

Today is Sunday

Current date is: 02/16/2014

Here we have used PHP's built-in *date* function to display the day of the week and current date. A function is a block of code that accomplishes a certain task. PHP's date() function is useful for getting date or time and depending upon the arguments provided, it displays date/time in different formats. Don't be scared with the terms function or argument, I don't expect you to understand those right now. We will cover these in a later chapter. For now, just run the above example and see how PHP can help you to dynamically generate output. Chapter 8 will be devoted to in depth discussion about functions.

date() is a built-in function to help you display date/time.

Summary

In this chapter we have started out\r programming journey and learned some foundational PHP skills. We ran our first "Hello World" program, we have learned how to output strings in PHP, how to insert PHP code blocks into HTML and finally how to comment PHP codes in order to make notes for programmers. Make sure you run each of the example programs provided in this chapter. I encourage you to type the code out by hand. Once you are comfortable with these topics, move on to the next chapter.

In the next chapter, we will learn about the concept of variables, data types, what different data types are offered by PHP, what are expressions, operators, operands and finally look at different operators available in PHP.

Chapter 6: Variables and Data Types

In previous chapter, we have learned some foundations about PHP. Now we know how to run simple PHP scripts that output strings to the browser. In this chapter, we are going to learn some other foundational concepts including the variables, data types, expressions and operators.

Variables

To put it simply, a variable is just a storage for a value. Since I haven't discussed about values yet, you can image of value as being a piece of data (like a number or a sequence of characters, we will discuss about values shortly). Let me give you an example -

```
$say_hello = "Hello World";
```

Here we assign (or store to put it simply) the value "Hello World" to the variable named $say_hello. From this point on, now we can refer to the variable $say_hello instead of the string (or character sequence) "Hello World". So, if we would like to output the "Hello World" string, we simply output the variable $say_hello -

```php
<?php
    $say_hello = "Hello World";
    echo $say_hello;
?>
```

If we run the above code, we will have the following output -

```
Hello World
```

A variable can be considered as a storage place for a value.

Variable Naming Conventions

There are few guidelines you need to follow while naming your variables -
- A variable always begins with a dollar sign ($), which is then followed by the variable name.
- Variable name can consist of one or more characters and must begin with a letter or an underscore.
- The remaining characters can be letters, numbers or underscore character.
- No space is allowed within variable names.
- Variable names are case sensitive, so $myVar is not the same as $MyVar or $myvar. The PHP interpreter recognizes them all as different variables.

You must follow the proper conventions while naming your variables.

Updating Value of a Variable

You can change the value stored in a variable at any point in time within your code. Further reference to that variable will use the updated value. Let's see an example -

```php
<?php
$x = 5;      //assign 5 to $x
$y = 10;     //assign 10 to $y

echo $x + $y; //this will output 15

echo "<br/>";

$x = 15;     //re-assign 15 to $x
echo $x + $y //this will output 25, because now $x=15 and $y=10
?>
```

Running the above code will result following output -

```
15
25
```

We initially assigned $x to 5 and $y to 10, that's why first echo statements output 15. Later we changed the value of $x and reassigned $x to 15. So we can see the second echo statement output the value 25.

You can reassign the value of variables within your PHP code. Further reference to that variable will hold the updated value.

Data Types in PHP

Data type simply refers to the type of value. PHP offers numerous data types for you, we will briefly look at the commonly used data types in this section.

Strings

By this time, you should already know what a string is. To recap, a string is just a sequence of characters. Whenever you want to use string in your PHP program, you always enclose them within two quotes. You can use either single quote or double quote -

```php
<?php
    //string enclosed in single quotes
    echo 'This is a single quoted string';

    echo "<br/>";

    //string enclosed in double quotes
    echo "This is a double quoted string";
?>
```

This will output -

This is a single quoted string
This is a double quoted string

We will discuss more about string in a later section. Strings are used a lot throughout PHP applications and they deserve it's own section!

71

Numbers

As you can already guess, numbers are numeric values. You have already seen numbers and you know there are whole numbers (we call it integers), fractional numbers and numbers with digits after decimal place (we call it floating point numbers). You can have positive numbers, as well as negative numbers. Also you can use E or e to represent scientific notation. Let's have a look at some examples -

```php
<?php
//assign int (short for integer) value to variable $x
$x = 65;
echo $x;
echo "<br/>";

//assign float (short for floating point numbers) value to variable $y
$y = 5.43;
echo $y;
echo "<br/>";

//assign of int value 6000 (written with scientific notation)
$z = 6E3;
echo $z;
?>
```

This will output -

```
65
5.43
6000
```

Numbers are numeric values, whole numbers are called int (short for integers) and fractional numbers are known as float (short for floating point numbers).

Boolean

The *boolean* data type is named after George Boole, a mathematician considered as one of the founding fathers of information theory. The boolean data type represents truth: with two values supported, **TRUE** or **FALSE** (case insensitive). You can use any non-zero value to represent **TRUE** and zero to represent **FALSE**.

```
$is_eligible = true;        //$is_eligible is true
$is_eligible = false;       //$is_eligible is false
$is_eligible = -1;      //$is_eligible is true
$is_eligible = 0;       //$is_eligible is false
$is_eligible = 15;          //$is_eligible is true
```

A boolean data type can be either true or false.

NULL

The **NULL** type represents "nothing". You may ask, how can a type represent nothing? Yes, it can be quite confusing at first, but later when you see a usage example of **NULL** type, it will make more sense. Essentially, when a variable is declared, but not assigned any value, then the variable has the type **NULL**.

```
$myVar;   //$myVar has NULL value
```

If you declare a variable, but don't assign any value to it, it will be of NULL type.

Array

Array is a compound data type, which allows multiple items of same type to be aggregated under a single entity. You can image an array as a collection of key/ value pairs. This means that, it maps keys to values. Let's consider an example. Say you have a shopping list. Your shopping list contains multiple items. You can use an array to represent your shopping list -

```
$items = array("milk", "fruit", "sugar", "tea", "chocolate");
```

Here first item of array is milk, second is fruit, third item is sugar and so on. If you haven't used an array, then you would have to use separate variables for each item like this -

```
$item1 = "milk";
$item2 = "fruit";
$item3 = "sugar";
$item4 = "tea";
$item5 = "chocolate";
```

Without an array, you had to use 5 different variables for storing 5 items. Consider what you would do if your shopping list had 20 or more items, you had to declare 20 separate variables in that case! But with an array, you can use a single variable to hold all the items. It not only facilitates you to use a single variable name instead of many variables, but when used with loops or other constructs (which we will learn in later chapters), it gives you more facility. So how do you refer to an item from an array?

```
echo $items[0];        //output first item (milk in this case)
echo $items[1];        //output second item (fruit in this case)
echo $items[2];        //output third item (sugar in this case)
echo $items[3];        //output fourth item (tea in this case)
echo $items[4];        //output fifth item (chocolate in this case)
```

We access array elements by *keys* (or indexes). We put square brackets after the array name and then use its index to access specific element of the array. While creating the array, we can specify the indexes explicitly, but the indexes are optional. In case you create array without specifying indexes, you can use numeric indexes starting from 0. So we use index 0 to access first array element, index 1 to access second array element and so on. In programming, we start counting from 0 instead of 1. In might some counter-intuitive but soon you will get used to this convention.

Array is a compound data type. You can consider an array as a collection of key-value pairs.

Expressions and Operators

An expression is basically a statement which represents a particular action in your program. A simple example is **1+2**. Expressions can be further broken down into operators and operands.

Operators are functionalities that perform some action, or in simple terms operate on values. This action can be anything, for example, if you have two numbers, then you can use addition operator to sum the two values and get the result. In this case, addition is an operator, which simply adds two values together. On the other hand, the two values used here are known as operands.

So operands are the values on which operators operate on. Let see few examples of operators and operands -

```
2 + 3;      //here + is the operator and 2 and 3 are operands
4 * 5;      //here * is the operator and 4 and 5 are operands
sqrt(9);    //sqrt is the operator and 9 is the operand
```

As you can see, an operator can be either a symbol or any keyword (in the above example, **sqrt** is an operator, which performs square root of the given number). The following sections will familiarize yourself with commonly used operators in PHP.

Operators can be defined as the functionalities that perform actions. Operands are the values on which operators operate on. Together, operators and operands construct expressions.

Arithmetic Operators

Let's start with simple arithmetic operators. We are all familiar with arithmetic operations from elementary school mathematics, like addition, subtraction, division and so on. PHP has operators for performing these operations. Let's see an example -

```
2 + 3;      //performs addition, result is 5
13 - 6;     //performs subtraction, result is 7
14 * 2;     //performs multiplication, result is 28
```

```
12 / 3;        //performs division, result is 4
```

It should be straight forward to all of you, since you all learned these basic arithmetic in grade 1 or grade 2.

Now, there is one other arithmetic operator which you might not have come across before. It is called the *modulus* operator (%). It returns the *remainder* of a division. Let's see an example -

```
17 % 3;        // gives reminder of dividing 17 by 3, which is 2
```

We can take two numbers and use any of the arithmetic operators. As we have learned about the concept of variables earlier, we can also use arithmetic operator to variables which holds numbers.

```
$a = 5;
$b = 3;
echo $a * $b;      //will output 15
$a = $b + 10;      //now the variable $a will contain the value 13
echo $a – 2;       //will output 11
```

PHP supports operators for common arithmetic operations.

The String Concatenation Operator

There is only a single string operator available in PHP, which is *concatenation* operator (but you have nothing to worry about, as PHP offers you a rich collection of build-in functions for manipulating string). String concatenation operator simply concatenate two strings together (or in simple terms, glue the two strings together). This operator is represented by period symbol (.) , let's see few examples -

```
echo "Hello". " world";//will output "Hello world"

$name = "Jack";        //assign string to variable
echo "Hello ". $name; //will output "Hello Jack"

$firstName = "John";
```

```
$secondName = "Smith";

// concatenate two string variables and store value in another variable
$fullName = $firstName . $secondName;
```

Pretty simple, right?

PHP has only one string operator which is the string concatenation operator.

Assignment Operators

Assignment operators are used to assign values to variable. There are a number of assignment operators, among which the simplest form of the assignment operator is used to assign a value to a variable, while the other operators do some operations before making the assignment. Let's have a look at few examples first -

```
$x = 9;                    //assign a number to variable $x
$hello = "Say Hello";   //assign a string to variable $hello
```

Equal sign (=) is the simplest form of assignment operator, which assigns a value to a variable.

Now let's consider we have a variable $x in our program. We want to increase the value of $x by 3 and re-assign the new value to $x. This can be done in the following way -

```
//add 3 to the previous value of $x and re-assign new value to $x
$x = $x + 3;
```

There is actually a shortcut assignment operator for this operation, which is addition-assignment operator -

```
$x += 3;    //addition-assignment
```

Similar shortcut assignment operators are also available for subtraction, multiplication and division -

```
$x = 11;     //assignment; $x is 11
$x += 4;     //addition-assignment; $x is 15
$x -= 3;     //subtraction-assignment; $x is 12
$x *= 5;     //multiplication-assignment; $x is 60
$x /= 6;     //division-assignment;     $x is 10
```

There is actually another assignment operator, which is string concatenation-assignment operator '.=', let's see an example -

```
//assignment, $msg contains "Hi there! "
$msg = "Hi there! ";
//concatenation-assignment, $msg contains "Hi there! How are you?"
$msg .= "How are you?";
```

You can use assignment operators to assign values to variables.

Increment and Decrement Operators

In programming, we often need to increment the value of a variable by 1 or sometimes need to decrement the value of a variable by 1 from the current value of that variable. PHP offers two shorthand operators, increment operator (**++**) and decrement operator (**--**) for these tasks.

```
$a = $a + 1;     //standard form, increment value of $a by 1
$a += 1;         //addition-assignment, also increment value by 1
$a++;        //shorthand for increment by 1
```
Similarly, you can use decrement operator -

```
$a--;        //will decrement current value of $a by 1
```

There are two variations of increment operator, pre-increment and post-increment, depending upon the increment operator is placed before or after the variable -

```
$a++;        //post-increment
++$a;        //pre-increment
```

Now you may ask what is the different between pre-increment and post-increment operator, aren't they both increase the value of $a by 1? Yes, you are right, both pre-increment and post-increment increases the value of the variable by 1, but when they are used in an expression, in case of pre-increment, the value of the variable is increased by 1 first and then new value is used in the expression. On the other hand, in case of post-increment, the current value of the variable is used in the expression and then value is incremented by 1.

Let's have a look at an example -

```
//pre-increment
$a = 4;          //assign 4 to $a
$b = ++$a;       //increase value of $a by 1 and assign new value to $b
echo $a;         //$a is 5
echo $b;         //$b is 5


//post-increment
$x = 4;          //assign 4 to $x
$y = $x++;       //assign value of $x to $y and then increase $x by 1
echo $x;         //$x is 5
echo $y;         //$y is 4
```

Now you can see the effect of using pre-increment and post-increment. Similarly you have pre-decrement and post-decrement operators as well.

```
//pre-decrement
$a = 7;          //assign 7 to $a
$b = --$a;       //decrease value of $a by 1 and assign new value to $b
echo $a;         //$a is 6
echo $b;         //$b is 6

//post-decrement
$x = 7;          //assign 7 to $x
$y = $x--;       //assign value of $x to $y and then decrease $x by 1
echo $x;         //$x is 6
```

```
echo $y;      //$y is 7
```

Increment or decrement operators provide shorthand for increase or decrease value of a numeric variable by 1.

Comparison Operators

Comparison operators are used to check the similarity between values. The result of a comparison between two values (or variables that contain values) is always a boolean (either **True** or **False**) value. Comparison operators are very useful in control structures to direct program flow (we will learn about control structures in the next chapter). Let's see different comparison operators with example -

Operator Symbol	Operator Name	Example	Outcome
==	Equal to, check for equality of value	2 == 2	True
===	Identical to, check for equality of value and type	2 === 2.0	False
!=	Not equal to	2 != 2	False
!==	Not identical to	3 !== 3.0	True
<	Less than	2 < 3	True
>	Greater than	2 > 3	False
<=	Less than or equal to	2 <= 3	True
>=	Greater than or equal to	2 >= 3	False

With comparison operators, you can check similarity between values.

Logical Operators

Like comparison operators, logical operators are useful with conditional statements to determine program flow. It's quite difficult to demonstrate the real usage of logical operators without control structures, but I will try to familiarize you with the logical operators here, so when we introduce conditional statements in the next chapter, we will have a better understanding of how these operators are used.

Logical AND

You can use **andand** (or alternatively **AND** keyword) as logical AND operator. Logical AND operator returns *True* if both expressions which are connected by AND operator are True.

expression1	expression2	expression1 andand expression2
True	True	True
True	False	False
False	True	False
False	False	False

Logical OR

The || symbol (or alternatively **OR** keyword) can be used as logical OR operator. Logical OR operator returns True if at least one of the two expressions which are connected by OR operator is True.

expression1	expression2	expression1 || expression2
True	True	True
True	False	True
False	True	True
False	False	False

Logical NOT

The ! symbol is used as logical NOT operator. This operator simply negates the truth value of preceding expression. So, if this operator precede any **True** expression, then that becomes **False**, on the other hand, if this operator precede any **False** expression, then that become **True**.

expression	!expression
True	False
False	True

Logical operators can be used with conditional statements to direct a program's flow.

Example: Calculating Area and Perimeter of Circle

Now let's go through an example to crystalize what we have learned about variables, operators and assigning values to them. Let's write a simple program to calculate the area and perimeter of a circle. If we have the radius of any circle, this program will calculate the area and perimeter. Let's see the code first -

```php
<?php
$radius = 3;
$pi = 3.14;
$area = $pi *(radius^2);
$perimeter = 2 * $pi * $radius;
echo "Radius of Circle: ".$radius;
echo "<br/>";
echo "Area: ".$area;
echo "<br/>";
echo "Perimeter: ".$perimeter;
?>
```

Now let's run the code and we will get the following output -

Radius of Circle: 3
Area: 6.28
Perimeter: 18.84

We store the value of radius in a variable called *$radius*, this enables us to use the variable name instead of the value of radius. We also store the value of PI in a

82

variable called *$pi*. Then we calculate the area and perimeter of the circle using respective formulas. While calculating area and perimeter, we referenced the variable $radius instead of using the value of radius. Now if you need to calculate the area and perimeter of another circle with different radius value, you just need to change the value of the variable $radius. If we didn't used variable, we had to change the value of radius in both of the statements where we calculate area and perimeter.

Summary

In this chapter, we have learned some other basic building blocks of PHP language (and programming in general). We have discussed about the concepts of variables, data types, expressions, operators and finally wrapped our discussion with an overview of commonly used operators in PHP. As we move through the next chapters, we will use these concepts to build interesting programs.

In the next chapter, we will discuss about control structures: conditionals and looping. Conditionals are used to determine program flow, while looping structures are used to repeat a task certain number of times or until a condition is meet. With the power of these constructs and building blocks we have learned so far, we will be able to develop useful programs. So if you are ready, let's move on to more fun stuffs!

Chapter 7: Control Structures –

Conditionals and Loops

In this chapter, we will learn about control structures. We will discuss about *conditional statements* which direct the flow of program based on different conditions. We will also learn about *looping constructs*, which are used to perform a task repeatedly or until a condition is fulfilled.

Conditionals

In our programs, we often need to perform a task if a specified condition is *true*, else we perform another task (the condition being *false* then). You can think about a real world scenario where our action vary depending upon the situation or condition. For example, if it is raining, we take an umbrella while going outside. In our PHP programs, we use conditional statements to check conditions and perform tasks accordingly. This approach of using conditional statements to direct flow of program enables us to embed logic within our programs.

With conditional statements, we can control the flow of programs and embed logic within our programs.

The 'if' Statement

The most basic form of conditional statement is the *if* statement. The if statement simply translates to: if the condition is true, then run the corresponding code block. It takes the following form -

```
if (expression) {
      //run this code block
}
```

The expression within the parenthesis is the condition, which evaluates to either true or false. The code block enclosed in the curly braces will run only if the expression evaluates to true (in other words, if the condition is true).

Let's consider an example: Suppose a bookstore is giving a 15% discount on purchase of books worth $200 or more. We can express this condition in PHP as follows-

```php
if ($total_amount >= 200) {
    $discount = 0.15 * $total_amount;
    $total_amount = $total_amount - $discount;
}

echo "You need to pay the amount: ".$total_amount;
```

Let me explain the previous example. The $total_amount variable holds the value of actual price of the books we have purchased. Within the *if* condition, we are checking whether we have purchased for an amount greater than or equal to $200 ($total_amount >= 200). If this condition is true, we then execute the two lines of code enclosed within the curly braces -
- At the first line, we calculate the discount and store the value within $discount variable. The value of $discount will be 15% of $total_amount.
- Then we apply discount to $total_amount. We simply deduct $discount amount from $total_amount and re-assign that value to $total_amount. At this point, $total_amount will be discounted price.

At the end of the *if* statement, we show a message to the customer regarding how much they need to pay. This line will be executed regardless of if condition is true or false.

Now, if the customer spend any amount less than $200, the *if* condition will be false and the corresponding code block will not be executed. The last line will output a message with the amount they need to pay.

On the other hand, if the customer spend at least $200, the *if* condition will be true and the corresponding code block will be executed, which will apply 15% discount to the $total_amount. Finally, after the *if* statement is executed, the last line of our program will output a message with the payable amount (the discounted price).

Now let's run the previous example for a purchase of amount $250 -

```php
<?php
$total_amount = 250;
```

```
if ($total_amount >= 200) {
      $discount = 0.15 * $total_amount;
      $total_amount = $total_amount - $discount;
}

echo "You need to pay the amount: ".$total_amount;
?>
```

If you run the above lines of code, you will get the following output -

> **You need to pay the amount: 212.5**

With the **if** statement, we can write a piece of code that will be executed only if a certain condition is true.

The 'else' Statement

As we have seen in the previous section, the *if* statement is useful for checking a condition and perform some action if the condition is true. Sometimes it is useful to provide an alternative action in case the condition is not met. We can use an *else* statement in case we want to have a block of code to be executed when the *if* condition is false.

```
if (expression) {
      //execute this code block when expression evaluates to true
}
else {
      //otherwise execute this code block
}
```

The above syntax tells that, if the expression evaluates to true, then run the corresponding code block, otherwise run the code within else block.

Let's have a look at the example below. Say we have program where users have to guess a secret number, if the guess is correct, then a congratulatory message will be displayed, otherwise we display a message to tell the user to try again.

```
<?php
$number = 25;
```

```php
$guess = 13;

if($number == $guess) {
    echo "Congratulations! You have correctly guessed the secret number!";
}
else {
    echo "Try again!";
}
?>
```

Now, if we run the above example, we will have the following output -

Try again!

You can see that we have a variable called $number which contains our secret number and $guess variable which represents the user's guess. Usually, we will get user's guess through HTML form and then access that using PHP's $_POST array, but since we haven't discussed about form processing with PHP till now, we have set the $guess variable by ourselves. Later we will learn how to pass data through *form* and how to access form data with PHP.

The **else** statement provides us the opportunity to execute a code block that will be executed when the **if** condition is not true.

The 'elseif' Statement

The *if-else* combination works fine where there are only two outcomes possible, that is an "either-or" situation. But often we will have to deal with several outcomes. With only if-else combination, we cannot deal with that. There is another statement "elseif" which can accomplish that task. You can use either "elseif" or "else if", both are allowed.

Using the *elseif* statement, we can improve our secret number guessing example discussed earlier. Previously we could handle two conditions only, whether the guess is correct or not. Now we can provide additional information to the user in case the guess is not correct. We can tell them whether their guess is smaller or greater than the secret number-

```php
<?php
```

```
$number = 25;
$guess = 21;

if($guess == $number) {
    echo "Congratulations! You have correctly guessed the secret number!";
}
elseif($guess < $number) {
    echo "Your guess is less than the secret number!";
}
else {
    echo "You have guessed a larger number than the secret number!";
}
?>
```

If we run the above example, we will have following output -

Your guess is less than the secret number!

Using the 'elseif' statement, we can provide alternative code blocks for conditions with more than two possible outcomes.

Using Logical Operators to Connect Multiple Conditions

There will be situations when we will need to evaluate multiple conditions and then based on the combined result of multiple conditions, perform a specific action. We can use logical operators (logical AND, logical OR) to connect multiple conditions. Let's say, you want to go for a tour if it is a holiday and when the weather is sunny. In this case, if both the conditions are met, only then you perform the task. You can use logical AND operator (*andand*) to express the above condition within your PHP code -

```
if($is_holiday == true andand $weather == "sunny") {
    //do some stuff here...
}
```

Let's consider an example, say we have a shop and we are running a campaign. Each customer who purchases a product during the campaign period will be given a coupon and we will give prizes to customers based on two conditions: if the

```
```

coupon has a serial number multiple of 101 and it is a holiday, only then will the customer win a prize. This condition can be expressed as follows -

```
if($coupon_serial % 101 == 0 andand $is_holiday == true) {
    echo "you win the prize";
}
```

Here we are using the logical AND operator (andand) to connect two conditions. Our first condition is the $coupon_serial need to be a multiple of 101, we express this condition as -

```
$coupon_serial % 101 == 0
```

If you don't recall the modulus operator (%) , then remind you again what it does. The modulus operator gives us the remainder of a division. If the reminder of dividing the $coupon_serial by 101 is equal to 0, then that means the $coupon_serial is a multiple of 101.

The second condition checks if it is a holiday (Let's consider we have a boolean variable $is_holiday which tell us if today is holiday or not) -

```
$is_holiday == true
```

We use logical AND operator (andand) to join two conditions, which returns True if and only if both the conditions are True. So if the $coupon_serial is a multiple of 101 and if it is a holiday, only then the combined condition will be evaluated as True.

Let's consider a case of the above example -

```
<?php
$coupon_serial = 301;
$is_holiday = true;

if($coupon_serial % 101 == 0 andand $is_holiday == true) {
    echo "you win the prize";
}

else {
    echo "sorry, try next time";
```

```
}
?>
```

If we run the above code snippet, we will get the following output -

> **sorry, try next time**

We can see that the condition of $is_holiday is true, but the other condition of $coupon_serial being multiple of 101 is false. So the combined condition evaluates to false and the corresponding else block is executed.

Similarly you can use logical OR (||) operator to connect multiple conditions within a conditional statement. But with logical OR operator, if any of two conditions is true, then the combined conditional statement will be evaluated as true. Let's see an example of using logical OR operator -

```php
<?php
$number = 15;

if($number > 50 || $number % 5 == 0) {
        echo "Then number is greater than 50 or a multiple of 5";
}
else {
        echo "The number doesn't match specified criteria";
}
?>
```

When we run the above example, we will get the output -

> **Then number is greater than 50 or a multiple of 5**

Here the first condition ($number greater than 50) is false, but the second condition ($number is a multiple of 5) is true. So the two conditions combined with logical OR operator (||) evaluates to true and corresponding code block is executed.

Logical 'AND' and Logical OR can connect multiple conditions. They enable us to evaluate more complex logic.

The switch Statement

The *switch* statement is another conditional statement available in PHP. A switch statement can be used as an alternative to a series of if statements on same expression. The switch statement is generally used in cases where you want to compare a variable or expression with a number of values and execute different code blocks depending on which value it matches.

The syntax of switch statement is as follows -

```
switch(variable) {
    case value1:
        //do something
        break;
    case value2:
        //do something
        break;
    case value3:
        //do something
        break;
    default:
        //do something
}
```

The default block is optional, if you want to provide a default code block in case none of the specified cases are matched, then you can use a default case.

Also notice the *break* statement at the end of each case. It is important to provide break statement at the end of each statement, otherwise if a match found with any of the specified case, then after the code block corresponding to that case is executed, all the remaining code will be executed as well.

Now let's write a program which will find the current weekday and output a different message to the user. We will write this example using both the *if* and *switch* statement. First we will see the *if* statement version of the program -

```
<?php

$weekday = date("D");

if($weekday == "Fri") {
    echo "Looking forward to weekend!";
```

```php
}
else if($weekday == "Sat") {
        echo "Enjoy your weekend!";
}
else if($weekday == "Sun") {
        echo "Happy Sunday";
}
else {
        echo "Wish you a good working day!";
}
?>
```

Now we will see how we can rewrite the above example using the *switch* statement -

```php
<?php

$weekday = date("D");

switch($weekday) {
        case "Fri":
                echo "Looking forward to weekend!";
                break;
        case "Sat":
                echo "Enjoy your weekend!";
                break;
        case "Sun":
                echo "Happy Sunday";
                break;
        default:
                echo "Wish you good working day!";
}
?>
```

The above example uses PHP's built-in date() function. The date("D") will return the three letters representation of current weekday (like Sat, Sun etc). You will learn more about functions in the next chapter.

Now run the above examples and you will be greeted with a message depending on the weekday that you run the example. Running the code snippet on Thursday gave me the following output -

> **Wish you good working day!**

You can also leave the statement list empty for some cases, this will simply pass the control into the statement list for the next case.

```php
switch($i) {
    case 1:
    case 2:
    case 3:
        echo "i is 3 or less";
        break;
    case 4:
        echo "i is 4";
        break;
}
```

Here, we have left the statements list for the first two cases empty. So if the value of variable $i matches either of the first two case, the statements associated with the next case will be executed.

The **switch** statement can be used as an alternative for a series of **if** statements on the same expression.

Looping Statements

Looping statements provide you the ability to repeat a set of instructions until a specific condition is satisfied. PHP provides several looping statements for performing tasks repeatedly (specified number of times or until a condition is met). The following sections discuss about different looping statements available in PHP.

The 'while' Statement

The *while* statement is the simplest type of looping statement available in PHP. With the while statement, we can specify a condition which must be satisfied before the execution of a code block is terminated. It has the following syntax -

```php
while (expression) {
    //do something
}
```

Let's consider a problem – say we are asked to calculate the sum of the numbers from 1 to 100. We can use a while loop to easily accomplish that -

```php
<?php
$total = 0;
$count = 1;

while ($count <= 100) {
    $total = $total + $count;
    $count++;
}

print "The summation of numbers from 1 to 100 is: ".$total;
?>
```

The above code will output -

The summation of numbers from 1 to 100 is: 5050

At first we initialize two variables, $total and $count. The variable $total is initialized to 0 and the variable $count is initialized to 1. Then we check the condition of while loop ($count <= 100) and if that condition is true, we do two things -
- Update the value of $total by adding $count to current value of $total
- Increment value of $count by 1

Since the initial value of $count is set to 1, when we first check the condition of while loop, it will be true. So we update value of $total by adding $count to current value of $total and then increment $count by 1. This will finish the first iteration of while loop. Then the condition of while statement will be checked again to see if $count is less than or equal to 100. If the condition is true, we again perform the above two steps. We repeatedly run this process until the condition become false. At one point, when the value of $count will be 101, then the condition of while statement will be false and the loop will stop.

With the each iteration of while statement, we have added the value of $count to the $total. We have started with the value of $count equal to 1 and then finally when have the value of $count equal to 101, the loop is terminated. But the last value of $count added to $total was 100, because we add the value of $count to $total and then increment $count. Thus we get the summation of numbers from 1 to 100.

Take particular attention to the second line within the body of the while statement ($count++). This line updates the condition of the while statement. If we don't include this line or instead of incrementing the value of $count, we decrement it ($count--), then the condition of while statement will always be true and the while loop will keep running forever. This type of loops are known as *infinite* loops. So make sure you update the termination condition accordingly and carefully to avoid unintentional infinite loops.

With the **while** statement, you can specify a condition which must be satisfied before the execution of the code block is terminated.

The do...while Statement

The *do...while* statement is actually a variant of the *while* statement. In case of the do...while statement, rather than checking the loop condition before the execution of the code block, the condition is checked after the execution of the code block. This ensures that, the code block associated with the do...while statement *will execute at least once*, even the loop condition is false.

The do...while statement has the following syntax -

```
do {
     statements
}
while (expression);
```

Let's have a look at an example. We have a variable named $count and we simply output the value of $count as long as the $count is less than 10. Using while statement, we can express this as follows -

```php
<?php

$count = 12;
```

```php
while ($count < 10) {
        echo $count;
        $count++;
}
?>
```

If you run the above code, you will get no output.

We can see the $count is initialized to 12. As a result, the loop condition will be false and the code block associated with while statement will never be executed. So we will get no output if we run the above code snippet.

Now let's use the do...while statement to write the same example -\

```php
<?php

$count = 12;

do {
        echo $count;
        $count++;
}
while ($count < 10);

?>
```

If we run the above code snippet, we will get the following output -

```
12
```

Even though the condition is false from the very beginning, the code block associated with do...while will run at least once. That is because of it checks the condition only after we execute the code block first.

The code block associated with a do...while statement will run at least once, even if the loop condition is false at the beginning.

96

The 'for' Statement

PHP offers another looping construct for performing a set of instructions repeatedly – the *for* statement. The syntax of 'for' statement is bit different from 'while' statement. Below is the syntax of for statement -

```
for(expression1; expression2; expression3) {
        statements
}
```

Let's have a closer look at what the expressions within the parenthesis are doing -
- expression1 is evaluated only once at the first iteration of the loop. We generally set the initial value of variable here.
- expression2 is evaluated at the beginning of every iteration. We check the loop condition here to determine whether loop will be continued or terminated.
- expression3 is evaluated at the end of each iteration. Typically, we update the value of the loop counter here.

Now we will see how we can rewrite the program for calculating the summation of numbers from 1 to 100 using the *for* loop -

```php
<?php
$total = 0;

for($count = 1; $count <= 100; $count++) {
        $total = $total + $count;
}

print "The summation of numbers from 1 to 100 is: ".$total;
?>
```

Once you run the above program, this will output -

The summation of numbers from 1 to 100 is: 5050

If you compare the above program with the while statement version of same program, then you can see we are doing the same steps here as we did with while statement. Let's see the how the steps of for statement can be compared with while statement -

- With the *while* statement, we initialized the $count before the loop, but with for statement, we initialized $count as expression1.
- The condition of while statement was checked within parenthesis, with for statement, we are checking condition as expression2.
- The $count variable was incremented within the body of while statement, in case of for loop, we are incrementing $count as expression3.

PHP offers another looping construct: the *foreach* statement, which is used to loop through arrays. The foreach statement will be introduced in next chapter, after we learn more about arrays.

With the **for** statement, you can execute a block of code a specified number of times.

The break Statement

The *break* statement can be used to terminate the execution of a loop immediately regardless of the loop condition. Whenever a break statement is encountered, it will stop execution of while, do...while, for, foreach, switch statements. Let's have a look at an example of using break statement in a *for* loop -

```php
<?php

for($i = 0; $i < 10; $i++) {
    $randomNumber = rand(1,20);

    if($randomNumber % 5 == 0) {
        break;
    }

    echo "The random number is: ".$randomNumber."<br/>";

}

?>
```

The rand() function returns a random integer within the specified range. So the rand(1,20) will return any integer between 1 and 20 (inclusive).

The above example uses random number generator function, so running this script will output different result each time. When I run the script, I got something like this -

```
The random number is: 8
The random number is: 17
The random number is: 14
The random number is: 4
The random number is: 9
```

Note that, though our loop condition was set to run 10 iterations, we only got 6 random numbers. That is because one of the random numbers generated was a multiple of 5. Thus the break condition was executed and the loop was terminated.

Run the above code by yourself. If no random number which is a multiple of 5 is generated, the loop will run for 10 iterations.

The **break** statement terminates the execution of a loop.

The 'continue' Statement

The continue statement causes the end of the execution of the current loop iteration, while other iterations of the loop will be executed as usual. Let's consider the same random number output example we have written in previous section, but with continue statement -

```php
<?php

for($i = 0; $i < 10; $i++) {
    $randomNumber = rand(1,20);

    if($randomNumber % 5 == 0) {
        continue;
    }

    echo "The random number is: ".$randomNumber."<br/>";
```

99

```
}

?>
```

Again, this example is using rand() function, so running this script will have a different output each time. Here is what I got when I run the example above -

```
The random number is: 11
The random number is: 3
The random number is: 9
The random number is: 11
The random number is: 12
The random number is: 3
The random number is: 1
The random number is: 14
```

In this case, when the random number is a multiple of 5, instead of terminating the loop, we simply end the current iteration of the loop, but keep running other iterations until the loop condition is satisfied. So if we have any random number multiple of 5, the continue statement will be executed and current loop iteration will be stopped. Then the next iteration of the loop will generate a new random number and if that number is not a multiple of 5, that number will be displayed.

The **continue** statement will terminate the execution of a current iteration of the loop; while it will keep running other iterations until the loop condition is satisfied.

Summary

We have learned about different control structures offered by PHP. Control structures enable us to use logic within our programs. Conditionals statements are useful for decision making, while looping constructs are useful for performing instructions repeatedly. The next chapter will discuss about the concept of functions. We will learn about defining your own functions, how to invoking functions, discuss about function arguments and other related concepts.

Chapter 8: Functions

In this chapter, we will learn an important concept of programming – *functions*. Functions are re-usable pieces of codes that perform a particular task. PHP language offers a huge number of built-in functions for accomplishing different tasks. We can also create our own functions. In this chapter, we will learn how to define our own functions, how to invoke functions, how to return values from function and other useful concepts related to functions.

The Concept of Functions

Programmers often write code which comprise of complex logic and there are situations when these codes can be reused frequently. For example, validating an email address is a very common task in web development. Consider a typical web application with a user account like a blog application. You will find that email address validation is required in many situations like user registration, updating user's profile, retrieve user's password and when someone subscribes to your blog posts. Now you can copy the email validation code to implement the above, but it is not a good approach. Your program file will contain duplicate codes, you can make mistakes while copying and pasting, or you might want to update your logic for validating email address at a later stage and realize that you need to update all the instances where you made the copy of the same codes. A better approach will be to define a function with the email valifation code block.

Essentially, a function is a named section of code. Whenever you identify that a block of code is doing a particular task and you might need to perform that task in other places, you might consider defining a function. PHP has a rich collection of built-in functions for many common web development tasks. Let's look at a couple of examples using PHP's built-in functions -

```
//perform square root of 9
echo sqrt(9);// will output 3

//returns the lowercase version of supplied string
echo strtolower("Hello World!");      //will output "hello world!"
```

A function is a reusable piece of code which performs a specific task.

Defining Your Own Functions

Although PHP provides an enriched collection of built-in functions, you will realize sooner or later that you need to create your own functions. When doing so, remember to avoid creating your own function if PHP already provides an existing one that performs your task. To define a function, you need to follow the below syntax -

```
function <functionName>(<parameters>) {
        function body...
}
```

Let me explain the syntax. We start with the "function" keyword, which is followed by the function name. After the function name, we provide the function parameters within the parenthesis. Parameters are data we provide to the function. Remember the square root function example we used earlier, sqrt(9)? Here, 9 is the parameter (or argument) provided to the sqrt() function). Some functions have more than one parameter, and some functions will have no parameter, but the parenthesis after the function name is mandatory. After the parenthesis, we will have the function body enclosed within the curly braces. This function body contains the code which will be executing once the function is invoked (function is called).

Let's define a simple function that outputs a message -

```php
<?php
function sayHello() {
        echo "Hello there!";
}
?>
```

Now, we invoke or call this function by its name -

```php
<?php
sayHello();
?>
```

Once PHP interpreter executes this line of code, the code inside the function body will be executed and you will get following the output -

Hello there!

Note that in the case of a user defined function, you need to put the function definition within the same file from where you want to invoke that function.

PHP provides you a huge collection of built-in functions, but also enables you to define your own function as needed.

Defining a Function with Parameters

We can define functions which accepts parameters. In the previous section, we have briefly discussed about function parameters. Function parameters are simply the data passed to the function. These data will be processed by the code inside the function body. As an example, let's define a function which calculates an item's total cost by adding tax to the price. We will pass two parameters, one for item's original price and the other the tax percentage.

```php
<?php
function calculateCost($price, $tax) {
    $tax_amount = $price * $tax;
    $total_amount = $price + $tax_amount;
    echo "Total cost is: ".$total_amount;
}
?>
```

Now if we want to invoke this function to calculate the cost of an item, we will need to provide the values for $price and $tax which are called function arguments. So you might have already guessed, function arguments are the values provided for the function parameters while invoking the function. Let's calculate the cost of an item of price $30 with 6% tax -

```php
<?php
$price = 30;
$tax = 0.06;
calculateCost($price, $tax);
?>
```

You could have passed the price and tax values directly instead of assigning them to variables -

```php
<?php
```

```
calculateCost(30, 0.06);
?>
```

Both the function calls will give the same output -

Total cost is: 31.8

We can pass data to functions as parameters.

Default Argument Values

You can define functions with default values assigned to input arguments. For these functions, if no argument is provided, a default value will be assigned to the argument. Let's define the calculateCost() function again with a default argument value for $tax as 7% -

```
<?php
function calculateCost($price, $tax=0.07) {
    $tax_amount = $price * $tax;
    $total_amount = $price + $tax_amount;
    echo "Total cost is: ".$total_amount;
}
?>
```

Now while invoking the calculateCost() function, we can only provide value for $price, in that case the default argument value of $tax will be used.

```
<?php
calculateCost(50);
?>
```

This will calculate the cost using default value of $tax (7%) and give the following output -

Total cost is: 53.5

We are also allowed to invoke this function will both arguments, in that case the default argument value will be overwritten by the supplied argument value.

```php
<?php
calculateCost(50, 0.11);
?>
```

Here the cost will be calculated using 11% as $tax and the function call will give the following output -

Total cost is: 55.5

You can provide more than one default argument value, but note that default argument values *must always appear at the end* of the parameter list.

You can also specify an optional argument by assigning an empty default value. Note that they must appear at the end of the parameter list as well.

```php
<?php
function totalPrice($price1, $price2="") {
        echo $price1 + price2;
}
?>
```
We can invoke this function with either both prices or with just $price1.

```php
<?php
totalPrice(10);          //will output 10
totalPrice(10,5);        //will output 15
?>
```

Both function calls are valid.

Sometimes we might want to make several arguments optional by providing them with empty default values -

```php
<?php
function totalPrice($price1, $price2="", $price3="") {
        echo $price1 + $price2 + $price3;
}
?>
```

While invoking this function, if we want to provide value of arguments $price1 and $price3, we can do this as well -

```php
<?php
totalPrice(45, "",12);
?>
```

The above function call will output-

57

You can define functions with default arguments values. Those arguments are then treated as optional.

Return Values from Functions

Within your function, you not only can perform tasks, but also return values back to the caller of the function (or caller scope. We talk about scope in a later section titled "Variable Scopes"). The "return" statement can be used to return values from a function. Let's have a look at calculateCost() function again. Now instead of output the total amount, we return that value -

```php
<?php
function calculateCost($price, $tax=0.07) {
      $tax_amount = $price * $tax;
      $total_amount = $price + $tax_amount;
      return $total_amount;
}
?>
```

Now once we invoke the calculateCost() function, we store the return value to a variable, and use it for any further calculation or simply output the value -

```php
<?php
$unit_price = calculateCost(45);
$num_units = 15;
$total_price = $num_units * $unit_price;
echo "The total cost for ".$num_units." items is: ".$total_price;
```

?>

This will output -

The total cost for 15 items is: 722.25

Explanation

We first calculate the price for a single item with tax using the calculateCost() function and then assign the return value to $unit_price variable. Next, we use that value to calculate the price of 15 pieces of that product and then finally output the total cost.

The **return** statement is used to return values from functions.

Recursive Functions

Recursive functions are functions that call themselves. Recursive functions are very powerful and can sometimes provide nice and elegant solutions for complex tasks. The idea behind a recursive function is that, you break a large complex problem into a number of simpler versions of the same problem.

Let us consider the example of calculating factorial. Recall that to calculate factorial of a number n, we multiplying all the numbers from n to 1 like the below formula illustrates,

$$factorial(n) = n * (n-1) * (n-2) * \ldots * 1$$

For example, factorial of 5 will be
$$factorial(5) = 5 * 4 * 3 * 2 * 1 = 120$$

Now we can solve the factorial calculation problem recursively. If we need to calculate factorial of 5, we can express that recursively as follows -

```
factorial(5) = 5 * factorial(4)        [factorial(5) as 5 * factorial(4)]
             = 5 * 4 * factorial(3)    [factorial(4) as 4 * factorial(3)]
             = 5 * 4 * 3 * factorial(2) [factorial(3) as 3 * factorial(2)]
             = 5 * 4 * 3 * 2 * factorial(1) [factorial(2) as 2 * factorial(1)]
             = 5 * 4 * 3 * 2 * 1        [factorial(1) as 1]
```

You can see that we are calculating factorial of 5. In the first step, we calculate factorial of 5 as 5 multiplied by factorial of 4. We then calculate factorial of 4 as 4 multiplied by factorial of 3 and we keep reducing the problem until we reach factorial of 1, which answer is known to us. Factorial of 1 is the *base case* here. At base case, we have the solution of the problem and we try to reduce the problem until it reaches its base case. Let's see how we can express this as code -

```php
<?php
function factorial($n) {
        if($n <= 1) {
                return 1;
        }
        else {
                return $n * factorial($n-1);
        }
}
?>
```

You can see we have an *if* condition, where we are checking if $n is less than or equal to 1. If that base case condition is true, we return 1 (because factorial of 1 is 1). If $n is greater than 1, then we return $n multiplied by factorial of ($n-1). We keep calling the factorial function recursively and each time the parameter gets smaller till at one point, the parameter will be reduced to 1 (base case). At that point, there will be no more recursive function call and the factorial of the initial number will be returned.

Now let's invoke the factorial() function to calculate factorial of 5 -

```php
<?php
echo "Factorial of 5 is: ". factorial(5);
?>
```

Which will output -

Factorial of 5 is: 120

Recursive functions are functions that call themselves. Using recursive

108

function, you break a complex problem into a number of same problems of smaller size.

Variable Scopes

We have learned about variables in the previous chapter. We have seen how we can declare variables within our PHP programs. In this chapter, while discussing about functions, we have used variables inside functions as well and also used variables as function parameters. You can declare variables anywhere in a PHP script. However, the location where a variable is declared is important, because the location of declaration of a variable greatly influences the scope in which a variable can be accessed. Generally speaking, PHP variables can have one of the following four scopes -

- Local variables
- Function parameters
- Global variables
- Static variables

Local variables

When you declare a variable within a function, it is considered as a local variable. This means that you can reference the variable in that function only. Even if you use the same named variable outside the function, that variable will be an entirely different variable from the one used inside the function.

```php
<?php
$x = 5;

function myFunc() {
      $x = 13;
      echo "x inside function: ".$x;
}

myFunc();
echo "<br/>";
echo "x outside function: ".$x;
?>
```
The above will output the following -

```
x inside function: 13
x outside function: 5
```

You can see two different values of $x are being output. This is because the $x inside the function is local to the function myFunc() and it has a lifetime during function execution time only, then it gets destroyed once the function execution completes.

A variable declared within a function has local scope.

Function Parameters

You can access the function parameters only within the function body. Once the function execution finishes, they are destroyed.

```
function squareNum($x) {
        echo $x * $x;
}
```

This function will output the square of a given number. Here, the function parameter $x can be accessed only inside the function, once the function execution is finished, it will be destroyed.

Function parameters are only accessible within its function body.

Global Variables

Global variables can be accessed in from any part of the program. However, if you want to access or modify a global variable in a function, you must explicitly declare that variable as *global* in that function. You use *global* keyword in front of the variable to declare that as a global variable.

```
<?php
$x = 6;
function myFunc() {
        global $x;
        $x++;
}
myFunc();
```

```
echo "x is: ".$x;
?>
```

This will output:

x is: 7

We have used the global keyword within the function myFunc() to tell the PHP interpreter that we are using the global variable $x within the function instead of creating a local variable. We then increment the value of $x by 1.

Alternatively we can use PHP's $GLOBALS array to access global variable from within any function. The previous example can be rewritten as follows -

```
<?php
$x = 6;

function myFunc() {
    $GLOBALS["x"]++;
}

myFunc();

echo "x is: ".$x;
?>
```

Which will output -

x is: 7

Though using global variables seems convenient, you should be aware that global variables can cause unexpected results if used without caution.

Static Variables

We have already seen that variables used within functions are destroyed once the function call execution is finished. But sometimes we may need to keep the value of a variable within successive function calls. For example, we might need to have

111

a function that automatically assigns numeric ids to different users. We can use static variables to keep track of the value of a variable within successive function calls. To declare a variable as a static variable, we simply use the *static* keyword before the variable name -

```php
<?php
function assignId() {
        static $id = 0;
        $id++;
        echo "You have been assigned the ID: $id<br/>";
}
?>
```

Now if we call the function for the first time, we will get the value of $id variable equal to 1. Further calls to this function will increment the $id by 1 each time. Let's see what will happen if we call this function 3 times -

```
assignId();
assignId();
assignId();
```

This will output -

```
You have been assigned the ID: 1
You have been assigned the ID: 2
You have been assigned the ID: 3
```

If we define a variable inside a function as static, the value of the variable will persist between function calls.

Summary

In this chapter, we have learned about functions which is one of the basic building blocks of modern programming languages. We have learned how to define functions, how to invoke functions, how to pass data to functions as arguments and other usages of functions.

Chapter 9: Strings and Arrays

While exploring different data types of PHP in Chapter 6, we learned about Strings and Arrays. In this chapter, we will discuss these two data types in detail and also discuss some of the built in functions for manipulating them.

Strings

By now, we already know that strings are sequence of characters. In PHP, we can specify strings in four different ways -
* single quotes
* double quotes
* heredoc syntax
* nowdoc syntax

Single Quoted Strings

You can specify a single quoted string by enclosing a sequence of characters within single quotes (').

```
echo 'This is a single quoted string.';
```

In case you need to put a literal single quote within your single quoted string, you need put an escape (\) before the single quote. Else the PHP interpreter will give an error.

```
echo 'What's your name?';
```

The above example shows a single quoted string with a literal single quote. If we run this code, it will give an error. Single quote (') acts as a string delimiter for single quoted strings and the PHP interpreter will not recognize that we are using the intermediate single quote as a string literal. We will have to explicitly tell the interpreter that we are going to use that single quote as a literal single quote, not as a delimiter. In this case, single quote is a special character and we need to escape this single quote. This process is known as escaping special characters. We can use backslash (\) to escape special characters. This is how it can be done -

```php
<?php
echo 'What\'s your name?';
?>
```

As you can guess, this will output -

What's your name?

Within the single quoted string, backslash (\) is also considered as a special character. So if you want to use a literal backslash (\) within single quoted string, you need to escape that as well -

```php
<?php
echo 'The backslash character is represented as \\';
?>
```

This will output -

The backslash character is represented as \

Notice we have used two backslashes. The first one is for escaping the literal backslash.

Within single quoted strings, literal single quote (') and backslash (\) characters are treated as special characters and they need be escaped using the backslash (\) character.

Double Quoted Strings

Like single quoted strings, you can enclose a character sequence with double quotes (").

```php
echo "This is a double quoted string.";
```

For double quoted strings, PHP interprets more escape sequences for special characters. More commonly used escape sequences are listed below

Escape Sequence	Meaning

114

\n	Newline
\t	Horizontal tab
\v	Vertical tab
\\	Backslash
\"	Double quote
\$	Dollar Sign

Let's see an example with dollar sign ($) used as string literal -

```php
<?php
echo "The price of the product is \$50";
?>
```

This will output -

The price of the product is $50

Within double quoted strings, variables are parsed (the variables are replaced by their values), but in the case of single quoted strings, variable names will not be parsed.

Let's see the example of using variable within single and double quoted strings. First we will see how single quoted string handles a variable within it -

```php
<?php
$name = "John";
echo 'Hello $name!';
?>
```

The above code snippet will output -

Hello $name!

We can see that the variable isn't parsed within the above single quoted string. Now Let's see what happens in the case of a double quoted string -

```php
<?php
```

```php
$name = "John";
echo "Hello $name!";
?>
```

This will output -

Hello John!

Within double quoted strings, escape sequences are interpreted as special characters and variables are parsed.

heredoc syntax

With heredoc syntax, you can output a large amount of texts. Instead of delimiting the string with single or double quotes, you use an identifier to mark the beginning and ending of a string. Let's have a look at an example below -

```php
<?php

$text = <<<EOF
PHP is the most popular language for web development. <br/>You can learn more
about PHP at <a href="http://www.php.net">PHP.net </a> .
EOF;

echo $text;
?>
```

This will output -

PHP is the most popular language for web development.
You can learn more about PHP at PHP.net .

Here we have used heredoc syntax to delimit a string and assigned that string to the variable $text. In the case of heredoc syntax, you should remember few things -
  • As I have already mentioned, instead of single or double quotes, an identifier

is used to delimit the string. You need to make sure that you don't use that identifier as part of your original string.

- We have used an identifier "EOF" to delimit the string in the above example.
- The opening identifier must be preceded with three left angle brackets (<<<).
- Parsing rules for heredoc are same as double quoted strings, so both variables and escape sequences are parsed within heredoc strings. But note that you don't need to escape double quotes.
- The closing identifier must start at the very beginning of the line, which means you must not use any other characters or spaces before the closing identifier.

You will usually use heredoc syntax in case you need to output a large amount of text block and you don't want to go through escaping of double quotes. For example, outputting a HTML code block might be a good candidate for using heredoc syntax.

The heredoc syntax is useful for outputting large block of texts without going through the trouble of escaping double quotes.

nowdoc syntax

PHP offers another syntax for delimiting the string which is very similar to heredoc syntax introduced in the previous section. The only difference is that with nowdoc syntax, PHP will not parse any of the text delimited by nowdoc syntax. In case of nowdoc syntax, the opening identifier is enclosed in single quotes. Let's have a look at the example below -

```
<?php
$str = <<<'EOF'
This is a nowdoc delimited string.
EOF;
?>
```

If you need to output a large block of text without the need for escaping, then you can use nowdoc syntax.

With nowdoc, PHP will not parse any text. So this syntax is useful if you want to output code snippets.

117

Commonly Used String Manipulation Functions

PHP has a number of built-in functions for manipulating strings. In this section, we will discuss about commonly used string manipulation functions.

Getting the String Length

Determining the length of a string is a common task. You can easily get the length of a string using the strlen() function. The strlen() function returns the length of the string. Let's see an example of strlen() -

```php
<?php
echo strlen("Hello World");
?>
```

This will output -

```
11
```

As the length of string "Hello World" is 11, the strlen() function returns 11 in the above example. Now let's see another example which demonstrates the usage of strlen() to get the length of password and then checks if the length of password is less than 6 characters. If the length of password is less than 6 characters, then it shows a message that password is invalid, otherwise it tells the user that the password is valid.

```php
<?php
$password = "mySecretPass";

if(strlen($password) < 6) {
        echo "Invalid password, provide at least 6 characters!";
}
else {
        echo "Valid password!";
}
?>
```

As we have the length of the password equal to 12 characters, if you run the above example, you will get the message -

```
Valid password!
```

strlen() function returns the length of a string

Getting a Substring

The substr() function returns a part of the string. You specifying the start position and optionally length of the substring you want -

```php
<?php
echo substr("Hello World", 6, 5);
?>
```

This will output-

World

The substr() function takes three parameters. The first parameter is the input string. The second parameter is the start position and the third parameter (which is optional) is the length of the substring.

In our previous example, we had the input string "Hello World". The start position is the index of character of input string from where we want to start our substring. Character index within string starts with 0, so within "Hello World", the "H" will have index 0, "e" will have index 1, first "l" will have index 2 etc. We want to get the second part "World", which starts with character "W" and the index of "W" within our input string is 6. So we set start position to 6. The third parameter, which is the length of the string is optional. We have specified the length as 5, so the resulting substring will contain 6 characters starting with "W".

With substr() function, you can get part of the string defined by starting position and length.

Getting the Position of a Substring

The strpos() function returns the position of the first occurrence of a substring within a string. If the substring isn't found within the string, 'false' value will be returned.

```php
<?php
```

```
echo strpos("Hello World", "World");
?>
```

This will output -

6

The first parameter is our input string and second parameter is substring we are looking for.

Striping Whitespaces away from a String

The trim() function is used to strip whitespaces from the beginning and end of the string.

```
$str = trim("        This is a string.        ");        //$str will contain "This is a string."
```

You can use ltrim() to strip whitespace from the beginning of string only. Similarly, rtrime() is used to strip whitespace from the end of the string.

Manipulating String Cases

You can use strtolower(), strtoupper(), ucfirst() and ucwords() to manipulate the case of the characters in your string.

Converting a String to Lowercase

If you want to get a string will all lowercase letters, you can use the strtolower() function -
```
<?php
$str = "This is a String!";
echo strtolower($str);
?>
```
This will output -

this is a string!

Converting a String to Uppercase

The strtoupper() function will return the uppercase version of the string passed in as argument -

```php
<?php
$str = "This is a String!";
echo strtoupper($str);
?>
```

This will output -

THIS IS A STRING!

Capitalize the First Letter of a String

If you want to capitalize the first letter of the script, you can use the ucfirst() function. However, if your string already contains some capital letters, they will be kept untouched as well -

```php
<?php
echo ucfirst("hello, How are you?");
?>
```

This will output -

Hello, How are you?

Capitalizing the First Letter of Each Word

You can use ucwords() function to capitalize the first letter of each word in a string -

```php
<?php
echo ucwords("What are you doing now?");
?>
```

You will get the following output -

```
What Are You Doing Now?
```

Arrays

An array in PHP is a collection of key/value pairs. Arrays in PHP are implemented using hash tables (hash table is simply a data structure which maps keys to values). Arrays can be used to group a collection of related items and group them under a single entity, though you can create an array with different types of items in PHP. Array keys (also known as indexes) can be either numerical or string type.

An Array is a collection of key/value pairs. Array items are accessed using keys (which are also known as indexes).

Creating an Array

You can create an array in several ways. The array() construct can be used to declare an array, the general form is shown below -

array([key1 =>] value1, [key2 =>] value2, [key3 =>] value3, ...);

The keys inside square brackets ([]) means that they are optional. In case you don't specify any keys, the items will be given numeric keys, starting from 0.

Let's have a look at concrete example of using array() construct -

$fruits = array("apple", "orange", "mango", "banana");

We have created an array named $fruits with four items. We haven't specified keys, so the first item "apple" will have the key 0, second item orange will have key 1 and so on. Let's see how we access array elements -

```
echo $fruits[0];    //will output "apple"
echo $fruits[1];    //will output "orange"
echo $fruits[2];    //will output "mango"
echo $fruits[3];    //will output "banana"
```

The array() construct can be used for creating an array.

We can also create an array by explicitly specifying indexes (an index is just an alternative name for array key). Let's see how we can create an array by explicitly specifying indexes -

```
$subjectsArr = array(
        "Jack" =>"Physics",
        "Mark" => "Biology",
        "Smith" => "Chemistry"
     );
```

We have created an array named $subjectsArr with student's name as indexes and subjects taken by students as values. Now let's see how we can access the elements of this array -

```
echo $subjectsArr["Jack"];        //will output "Physics"
echo $subjectsArr["Mark"];        //will output "Biology"
echo $subjectsArr["Smith"];       //will output "Chemistry"
```

An alternative way to create an array is to specify the items -

```
$names[] = "Jacob";
$names[] = "Richard";
$names[] = "Charles";
```

This will create a new array called $names with three elements. Since we haven't specified the keys, the values will have numeric keys, starting from 0. The previous example can be rewritten by specifying the indexes as follows -

```
$names[0] = "Jacob";
$names[1] = "Richard";
$names[2] = "Charles";
```

Similarly we can create an array with string indexes as well -

```
$arr["key1"] = "value1";
$arr["key2"] = "value2";
$arr["key3"] = "value3";
```

The array items can be of any data type. It is common that you see an array consisting of values of different data types -

```
$info["name"] = "Jordan";
$info["age"] = 26;
$info["is_qualified"] = true;
```

Here, we have created an array called $info which has three items. The first item with index "name" has a value of string type. The second item with index "age" has a value of integer type and the third item with key "is_qualified" has a value of type boolean.

We can create arrays with mixed data types.

Printing the Items in Arrays

While working with arrays, you will often need to output the contents of an array for testing purposes. If you have already tried echo to output the array, you might have noticed that it doesn't work for arrays. PHP provides you the print_r() function for outputting array content. It will organize array contents to a readable format. Let's consider an example -

```
<?php
$fruits = array("apple", "orange", "mango", "banana");

print_r($fruits);
?>
```

This will output -

```
Array ( [0] => apple [1] => orange [2] => mango [3] => banana )
```

Note that if you wrap the print_r() function call with HTML <pre> tag, you will get a more readable format -

```
<?php
$fruits = array("apple", "orange", "mango", "banana");

echo "<pre>";
```

```php
print_r($fruits);
echo "</pre>";
?>
```

The output will be -

```
Array
(
    [0] => apple
    [1] => orange
    [2] => mango
    [3] => banana
)
```

print_r() function wrapped within <pre> tags can be used to output array items in a readable format.

Using range() Function to Create Arrays

You can use range() function to create an array with specified low and high integer values -

```php
<?php
$numbers = range(1, 5);

echo "<pre>";
print_r($numbers);
echo "</pre>";
?>
```

This will output -

```
Array
(
    [0] => 1
    [1] => 2
    [2] => 3
    [3] => 4
    [4] => 5
)
```

range(1,5) can also be specified as follows -

$numbers = array(1, 2, 3, 4, 5);

The range() function can take an optional third argument which specifies the step -

```
<?php
$numbers = range(1, 12, 2);

echo "<pre>";
print_r($numbers);
echo "</pre>";
?>
```

This will output -

```
Array
(
    [0] => 1
    [1] => 3
    [2] => 5
    [3] => 7
    [4] => 9
    [5] => 11
)
```

The range() function can be used for character sequences as well -

```php
<?php
$characters = range("A", "F");

echo "<pre>";
print_r($characters);
echo "</pre>";
?>
```

Which will output -

```
Array
(
    [0] => A
    [1] => B
    [2] => C
    [3] => D
    [4] => E
    [5] => F
)
```

The range() function can create an array of numbers (or characters) by specifying start and end numbers (or characters).

Adding and Removing Array Elements

You can add or remove elements from both the front and end of the array. The below sections show you how you can do that.

Adding Element to front of Array

You can use the array_unshift() function to add new elements to the front of array -

```php
<?php
$fruits = array("apple", "orange", "mango");
array_unshift($fruits, "banana");
```

```php
echo "<pre>";
print_r($fruits);
echo "</pre>";
?>
```

This will output -

```
Array
(
    [0] => banana
    [1] => apple
    [2] => orange
    [3] => mango
)
```

We can see that a new element "banana" is added to the front of array.

We can use array_unshift() to add new elements to the front of an array.

Removing Element from Front of Array

The array_shift() function removes the first element of the array and returns that element -

```php
<?php
$fruits = array("apple", "orange", "banana");
$firstElement = array_shift($fruits);

echo "Item removed: ".$firstElement;
echo "<br/>";

echo "<pre>";
print_r($fruits);
echo "</pre>";
?>
```
This will output -

```
Item removed: apple

Array
(
    [0] => orange
    [1] => banana
)
```

Here, we have assigned the return value of array_shift() to a variable. We can see that after the call to array_shift() the first element of the array is removed from the array and assigned to that variable.

array_shift() not only removes the first element of array, it also returns the removed element.

Adding Element to the End of Array

The array_push() function is used to add new elements add the end of the array -

```php
<?php
$fruits = array("apple", "orange", "mango");
array_push($fruits, "banana");

echo "<pre>";
print_r($fruits);
echo "</pre>";
?>
```

This will output -

```
Array
(
    [0] => apple
    [1] => orange
    [2] => mango
    [3] => banana
)
```

In this case, the new element is added to the end of the array.

Removing an Element from the end of Array

The array_pop() function removes the last element of the array and returns that element -

```php
<?php
$fruits = array("apple", "orange", "banana");
$firstElement = array_pop($fruits);

echo "Item reomoved: ".$firstElement;
echo "<br/>";

echo "<pre>";
print_r($fruits);
echo "</pre>";
?>
```

This will output -

```
Item reomoved: banana

Array
(
    [0] => apple
    [1] => orange
)
```

In this case, we have assigned the return value of array_pop() to a variable. We can see that after the call to array_pop(), the last element of the array is removed from the array and assigned to that variable.

element.

Getting Number of Items in an Array

We can easily get the number of items in an array. The count() function returns the item count of an array -

```php
<?php
$fruits = array("apple", "orange", "mango", "banana");
echo count($fruits);
?>
```

This will output -

4

With count() function, we can get the number of items in an array.

Looping through Array Elements

We have already learned about looping constructs of PHP like the for loop, while loop and do...while loop. We can also use these constructs to loop through array elements. Let's see an example of using the for loop to output array elements -

```php
<?php
$fruits = array("apple", "orange", "mango", "banana");

for($i=0; $i < count($fruits); $i++) {
    echo $fruits[$i];
    echo "<br/>";
}
?>
```

This will output -

```
apple
orange
mango
banana
```

But there is another loop which is dedicated for looping through the arrays – the 'foreach' loop. Let's see how we can rewrite the previous example using the foreach loop -

```php
<?php
$fruits = array("apple", "orange", "mango", "banana");

foreach($fruits as $fruit) {
      echo $fruit;
      echo "<br/>";
}
?>
```

Which will output the same result as the previous example.

With a foreach loop, we can also get the array keys as well. This is particularly useful for non-numeric keys. Let's have a look at the below example -

```php
<?php
$subjectsArr = array(
                  "Jack" =>"Physics",
                  "Mark" => "Biology",
                  "Smith" => "Chemistry"
            );

foreach($subjectsArr as $key=>$val) {
      echo "Student: $key, Subject: $val<br/>";
}
?>
```

This will output -

```
Student: Jack, Subject: Physics
Student: Mark, Subject: Biology
Student: Smith, Subject: Chemistry
```

You can see how conveniently we can loop through an array using the foreach construct.

The foreach construct is used to loop through an array.

Example: Using Array to Populate a Drop-down List

In this example, we will see how we can use an array to generate drop-down lists dynamically to our HTML forms -

```php
<?php
$states = array("Alabama","Alaska","Ohio","Pennsylvania","New York",);
?>

<form>
     Select State:
     <select name="state">
     <?php
          foreach($states as $state) {
               echo "<option>$state</option>";
          }
     ?>
     </select>
</form>
```

Say we have an HTML form and we would like to let the user choose the states of US from a drop-down list. Without using an array, we will need to add 50 different options for 50 states to our drop-down list. But using PHP, we store all the states in an array called $states (in our example, we have only 5 states as a sample, but in real usage, it will hold 50 state names). Then using a foreach loop, we go through each state names and create the option names dynamically. See how easily we can do tedious things with PHP.

Using the PHP Manual

The PHP Manual available at the official website of PHP (php.net) is an excellent resource for learning PHP. It has extensive documentation about all aspects of PHP language. Visit the website at http://www.php.net/ and go to the documentation section. The documentation is translated to multiple languages. You can either read the manual online or download for offline use. Alongside many other useful things, the PHP Manual has a section called "Function Reference", which has reference to all the available functions. Check those sections to learn more about different useful functions. For example - you can learn more string and array functions at -

http://www.php.net/manual/en/ref.strings.php
http://www.php.net/manual/en/book.array.php

Take time to make yourself familiarize with the documentation section, you will find the informations are well organized and very useful.

Summary

In this chapter we discussed about strings and arrays in detail. Along the way, we have learned about few useful functions for manipulating both strings and arrays. In the next chapter, we will learn how to process HTML forms with PHP.

Chapter 10: Form Processing With PHP

HTML forms are the main point of interaction between users and your website. In this chapter, we will learn about how we can access form data using PHP. This will enable us to do all sorts of interesting things like getting feedback from users, facilitate forum conversations, online ordering systems and so on.

Processing HTML Forms

Accepting user inputs through HTML forms is a two-step process. First we accept user input through HTML forms and process the input using a server side programming language like PHP.

The PHP language greatly simplifies the process of handling HTML forms. In fact, the way it handles HTML forms is one of the most powerful features of PHP. Any form element is automatically available in your PHP scripts. Let's have a look at an example of how simple it is you can handle HTML forms with PHP. First, we need to create an HTML form -

```
<form method="post" action="process.php">
Enter Your Name: <input type="text" name="name"/><br/>
Enter Your Age: <input type="text" name="age"/><br/>
<input type="submit" name="submit"/>
</form>
```

Save this file as *form.php* and put it under the web server (*htdocs* folder). We have a form with two *text* input elements and a *submit* button. The first *text* input element is for getting the user's name and the second text input element for age. Note that the opening form element has two attributes, **"method"** and **"action"**. The **method** attribute specifies which HTTP method will be used for submitting the form (more on this later). The **action** attribute specifies where to submit the form. In our example form, we have specified the "process.php" page as **action**, so the form submission will be handled by "process.php" page. Now let's create this process.php page to handle our form submission -

```
<?php
echo "Hello ".$_POST["name"].", you are ".$_POST["age"]. " years old!";
?>
```

Save this as process.php under the same directory where you have put form.php file. Here, we output a single line with the name and age entered by the user from the HTML form. As we have used "post" as the form's **method** attribute, we can get the value entered into the *name* field using $_POST["name"] and get the value of *age* field using $_POST["age"]. Let's run the form.php file from our local server (http://localhost/form.php) -

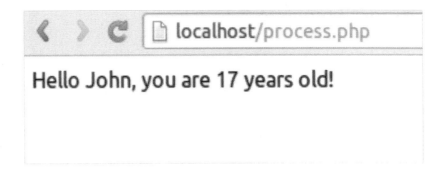

Now, enter the values of name and age and submit the form. Once you submit the form, you will see something like the below (but instead of name "John" and age "17", you will see the value of name and age entered by you) -

You will notice that once you submit the form, you will be taken to a new page (if you check browser's address bar, you will see http://localhost/process.php). This is because we have told our HTML form to send our form data to "process.php" page by setting **action** attribute to "process.php".

To accept user inputs through forms, in addition to creating HTML forms, you need to handle form submission using server side language like PHP.

The GET and POST Methods

The **method** attribute of <form> tag can have one of two methods: GET and POST (note that they are case insensitive). Once the form is submitted, the PHP file specified by **action** attribute can access the form fields. Depending on which **method** you specify using the form's **method** attribute, the form handling PHP file can access the form's fields using the array **$_GET** or **$_POST** (for GET and POST methods respectively).

The POST Method

If your form's method attribute has the value "post", then once the form submitted, the form processing PHP script will have access to an array called $_POST. This $_POST array will be populated with all the form elements in the form of key-value pairs, where the keys will be the **name** attributes of corresponding form elements and values will be the user inputted values to those form fields. Let's use our previous form example again to examine the $_POST array closely -

```
<form method="post" action="process.php">
Enter Your Name: <input type="text" name="name"/><br/>
Enter Your Age: <input type="text" name="age"/><br/>
<input type="submit" name="submit"/>
</form>
```

Now in process.php, let's output the $_POST array using the print_r() function -

```
<?php
echo "<pre>";
print_r($_POST);
echo "</pre>";
?>
```

If we submit the above form with the value for name field "John" and age field "17", we will see the $_POST array's elements as follows -

```
Array
(
    [name] => John
    [age] => 17
    [submit] => Submit
)
```

Our HTML form has two text input with name attributes "name" and "age". The submit button has name attribute of "submit". We see that the output of $_POST array has three elements with keys "name", "age" and "submit". In case of "name" and "age" keys, the corresponding values are obtained from user input and the "submit" key has a default value of 'Submit'.

If the form's **method** is set to "post", we can access the values of form elements using PHP $_POST array.

The GET Method

Now we will see how we can access the user input of the same form using GET method. Here is the HTML code for our form -

```
<form method="get" action="process.php">
Enter Your Name: <input type="text" name="name"/><br/>
Enter Your Age: <input type="text" name="age"/><br/>
<input type="submit" name="submit"/>
</form>
```

We have only updated the line in **bold**. Specifically, we just changed the value of method attribute from "post" to "get". Next, update process.php file with the following code -

```
<?php
echo "Hello ".$_GET["name"].", you are ".$_GET["age"]. " years old!";
?>
```

Note that now, we are accessing the input values using $_GET array. If we submit the above form with sample input "John" as name and "17" as age, then we will get following output -

138

Hello John, you are 17 years old!

If you look at the browser's address bar, you can see the URL -

http://localhost/process.php?name=Johnandage=17andsubmit=Submit

We have specified action attribute of the form as "process.php", but we can see some other additional data to the URL -

name=Johnandage=17andsubmit=Submit

This is exactly the key-value pairs in the $_GET array. In the case of GET method, the form's data are displayed in the URL in the form -

key1=value1andkey2=value2

This is known as a query string. In the case of GET method, all the forms input values are appended to the URL in the form of a query string.

The HTML form input with form's **method** set to "get" can be accessed using $_GET array.

GET vs POST

Though you can use either GET or POST method to your HTML form, they are not meant to be used interchangeably. The GET method is usually used to request or retrieve data, whereas the POST method is used for storing or updating data. The general rule is, if the processing of the form is security sensitive (in other words, you are ok if the information is known to others), you should use GET method. On the other hand, if the data in the processing of form is sensitive data, you should use POST method.

If you submit a form with GET method, all the form field data will be visible to the browser's URL as query string. So, if your form has fields for sensitive data like password or credit card information which you don't want to expose to others. In that case you should not use GET method, you should instead use the POST method.

Form submitted with POST method doesn't expose the form field data as query string, so you cannot bookmark the resulting page of POST requests. Database searches, like product search or something similar to that are appropriate when you want to bookmark the resulting page. In those cases, you might want to use GET method.

Also, in the case of GET requests, form data is passed through URL as a query string. So you should consider the fact that there is a limited amount of data being allowed to pass through the URL. That's why forms that pass large amount of data should use POST method.

GET method is appropriate for retrieving data while the POST method is appropriate for submitting data.

Summary

In this chapter we have learned how we can get user's input through HTML forms and also how to process them using PHP language. The next chapter will give us an introduction to *MySQL*, the database server we will be using for storing data for our websites.

Chapter 11: Introduction to MySQL

In this chapter we will learn about the concepts of Databases which is an important component for dynamic websites. We will learn about the *MySQL* database. Along the way, we will learn basic database terminologies and how to do basic operations like creating databases and tables. We will also learn how to do operations like data insertion, update, delete and retrieval.

What is a Database?

A database is an organized way to store data enabling you to easily retrieve and manipulate the store data. Whether you want to build a website for your online store or your personal blog, you will need to store relevant data like product information, customer information, purchase details and blog articles. Using a database, you can access and manage these data with ease.

A database is hosted on a database server. A database server is a software program that gives access to your databases. There are many database servers available. Some the popular database servers are MySQL, Oracle, MSSQL and PostgreSQL. In this chapter, we will be learning about MySQL, a very popular choice among the PHP developers community.

Database is an organized way to store data. It gives easy access to retrieve and manipulate data.

Why We Should Use a Database?

Suppose we want to build a blog website. Without using a database, we can create a bunch of HTML pages for the blog articles and upload those pages. But every time we want to publish a new blog article, we will have to create and design a new HTML page. Now let's see why this approach isn't good. If we want to update the design, we will have to go through every HTML page to make changes (though using a common CSS file, we can change the styles, but what if we need to update the structure of the pages?). Also, how we can categorize the blog articles for better accessibility? How will we enable readers of our blog to make comments? Where we will store those comments and then them alongside the corresponding articles?

However, if we use a database to store data for our blog, we no longer need to create separate HTML pages for each article. Instead, we will create a common template page for displaying blog articles. The actual blog article contents (article title, article description, publication date etc) will be stored n database and we will use an identifier to uniquely identify each article. We can then use PHP to retrieve the content of each article from the database and create a unique page for each article dynamically using the common article page template. So you can see the same article template page can generate dynamic pages for each article by incorporating article information retrieved from the database. Similarly, we can store blog comments in the database and keep track of which corresponding article for which the comment was made using an identifier. We can then retrieve the comments later on and display them to their corresponding article using that identifier. Moreover, we can incorporate search functionality in our blog querying from the database and filtering the results to serve our users better.

Introduction to MySQL

MySQL is an open source database server which is very popular among PHP developers. Before working with MySQL, you need to install it on your development machine. If you have followed the instructions provided in chapter 2 to install XAMPP, then you should have MySQL installed on your local development environment. Otherwise, revisit chapter 2 to make sure your database server is properly installed and running.

To access and administer MySQL, you will need a client program. There are both 'command line' and 'graphical user interface' based client programs. We will use *phpMyAdmin*, which is the most popular client program to administer MySQL from the web using a nice graphical user interface. *phpMyAdmin* is bundled with the XAMPP package. So if you have installed XAMPP, you can access the phpMyAdmin from your local server using the following URL -

http://localhost/phpmyadmin/

This will take you to the login page of phpMyAdmin -

142

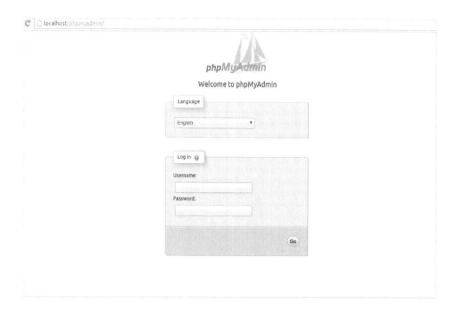

To login, use the default administrator account with username "root" and leave the password blank -

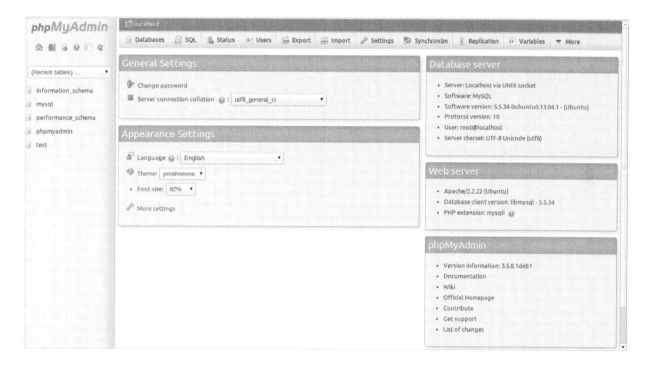

Once you login, you will see the wide range of operations that can be performed to manage and administer MySQL. Try to explore the different options. We will go through the major options later.

phpMyAdmin provides a web interface to administer your MySQL database.

Structured Query Language

Structured Query Language or **SQL** is the language used for interacting with MySQL database. In fact, SQL is the standard language for interacting with most other database software. Using SQL commands, we can do all sorts of database operations, like creating databases and tables, querying tables, inserting new rows to tables, deleting rows, updating tables and so on.

Using phpMyAdmin, we can perform database administration and other operations without using SQL commands. But from within our PHP files, we will have to write SQL commands to interact with MySQL database. That's why we need to learn SQL commands. We can also execute SQL commands from phpMyAdmin as well. In the following sections, we will see how to create tables, insert/edit/delete rows, query records etc. We will learn both SQL commands and also see how to use phpMyAdmin for these tasks.

Creating a Database

First of all, we need to create a database. Within our MySQL database server, we can create multiple databases. Typically, we create a separate database for each project. Now let's see how we can create a new database. First we will use phpMyAdmin to create our database. Then we will see the SQL command used for creating a new database.

Using phpMyAdmin

First login to phpMyAdmin by accessing the URL http://localhost/phpmyadmin/ , then from the top navigation option, click "Databases", then you will see the option to create a new database along with all the available databases -

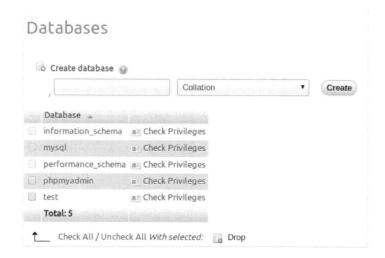

Now enter the database name to the form field and then submit the "Create" button. Your new database will be created.

Using SQL Command

Now we will look at the SQL command to create a new database. Before that, let's see how we can execute SQL commands from within phpMyAdmin. From the top level navigation menu, click "SQL" tab and you will see a window like this -

You will have to execute your SQL commands from within this window.

Now, the SQL command for creating a database is -

CREATE DATABASE <databaseName>;

<databaseName> is the name of the database you will want to create. The SQL commands are case-insensitive and ends with semicolon (;) . So if you want to create a new database named "blog", you will execute the following SQL

145

command -

CREATE DATABASE blog;

Enter the above command to the phpMyAdmin window and then press the "Go" button. Your new database will be created.

Database Tables

A database is composed of one or more tables. Items within a database are stored in these tables. A table contains a list of related items. For example, our blog application might have two tables: one table for blog posts and another table for comments. Each database table has a number of fields or columns, where each column holds a particular piece of information about the item that table holds. Our blog posts table might have columns like – title of the post, post content, publication date etc. Each blog post you save in your database table will be called a row or entry.

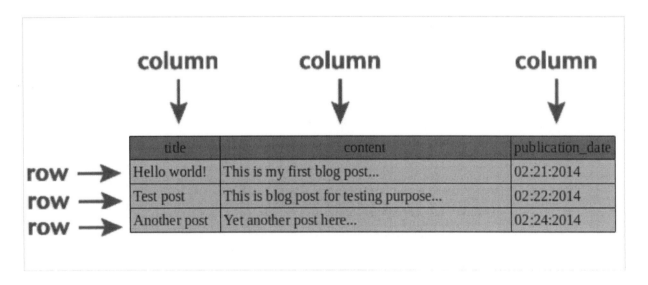

Here you can see our table has three columns (title, content, publication_date) and also three rows.

Creating Tables

Now let's see how we can create our first table. We will see both the SQL command approach and phpMyAdmin interface for creating the table.

Using SQL Commands

The basic form of SQL command for creating table looks like this -

```
CREATE TABLE <tableName> (
    <column1> <column1Type> <column1Details>,
    <column2> <column2Type> <column2Details>,
    <column3> <column3Type> <column3Details>,
    ...
);
```

The SQL command starts with 'CREATE TABLE' followed by the table name and the table description within the parenthesis. The table description typically consists of the column information of the tables, where each column information consists of column name, column data type and optionally some other details. Each column information is separated by comma.

Now let's create a table for storing articles. We will create a table named "article" with four columns, id, title, content and publication_date. Let's have a look at the SQL command for creating our article table -

```
CREATE TABLE article (
    id INT PRIMARY KEY AUTO_INCREMENT,
    title VARCHAR(250),
    content TEXT,
    publication_date DATE
);
```

Let me explain the SQL command written above.

CREATE TABLE article

This part of the SQL command tells to create a table called "article". The rest of the create statement within the parenthesis describe the table columns. We have four columns. Let's go through each of them -
id INT PRIMARY KEY AUTO_INCREMENT,

Here we have defined a column named "id" of type integer (which is defined by using the keyword INT after the column name). Next, we have other additional attributes. The keyword "PRIMARY KEY" tells the database table that, this column will act as the unique identifier for the entries of this table, so all the values of this column will be unique (the unique identifier enables us to locate a specific row. For e.g. the unique identifier for students in a school will be their student id. For books in a store, it will be their ISBN number). Finally we have the keyword "AUTO_INCREMENT" which tells the table to pick an id automatically in case we don't provide an id value. In that case, it will assign a value which is one more than the highest value in the table so far. E.g. the existing id is 10, the next id provided by 'AUTO_INCREMENT' will give 11.

title VARCHAR(250),

Here the column "title" of data type VARCHAR is defined. VARCHAR is a data type which hold string values of variable length. In the case of VARCHAR data type, we need to specify the maximum size of the string. In our case, we have 250 as the size of the string. The maximum size of VARCHAR can be 255. For larger chunks of text values, we will use the type TEXT.

content TEXT,

This column called "content" will hold the actual article texts. It has a data type of TEXT, which can hold string of any length.

publication_date DATE

The column "publication_date" will hold data of type DATE.

Now go to your phpMyAdmin panel and from the left side panel, click the database name you have created in previous step (the blog database).

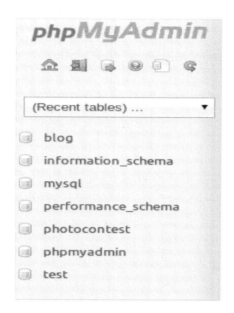

Once you select the blog database, go to "SQL" tab from the top navigation bar and execute the SQL command for creating our article table. Your table will be created.

Using phpMyAdmin Interface

You can also create the table without using SQL command by using the phpMyAdmin graphical interface. To do so, select the database following which you will see the following screen -

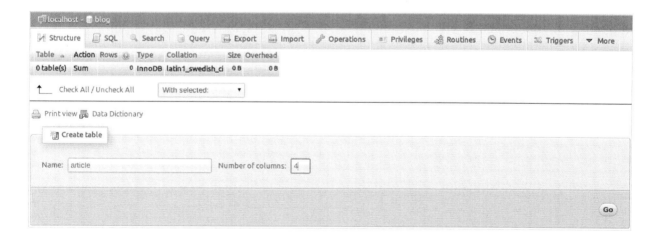

Under the "Create table" option, give the name of table and number of columns, then click "Go" button. The next screen will give you option to set your table columns -

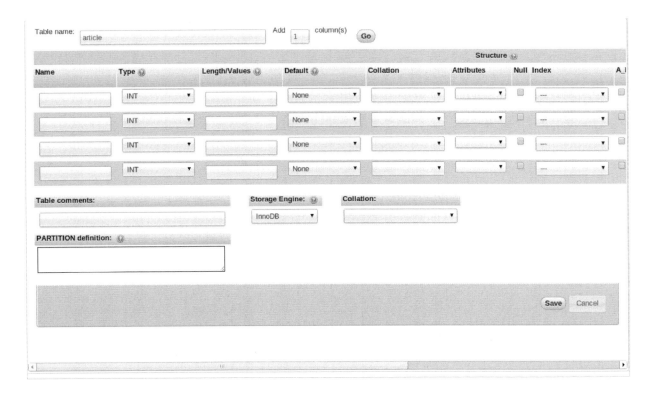

You will see a form like the above one to set your column names and attributes. The 'name' field will hold the column name. You can select data type of the column from the 'type' drop-down list. From the 'Index' drop-down list, you can select 'Primary Key' for id column. The 'A. I.' column next to 'Index' has a check box (A.I. stands for auto-increment). If you check that box, the column will have the auto increment attribute (you will check this box for id column). Once you are done, click the "Save" button to create the table.

Insert Data into Table

Now that we have created our table, let's see how we can insert data into it. First, let's see the SQL statement for inserting data.

SQL Insert Command

The SQL command for inserting data into a table has the following general form -

INSERT INTO <tableName>
(column1, column2, column3, ...)
VALUES (column1Value, column2Value, column3Value, ...);

Here we can see, we use the keyword "INSERT INTO", which is followed by *tableName*. Then within the parenthesis, we list the column names which are then followed by the values for those columns in the latter parenthesis.

Now let's see how we can insert a new record to our 'article' table -

INSERT INTO article
(title, content, publication_date)
VALUES ("my title", "content goes here", "2014-03-01");

Notice that, we have not provided the value for 'id' column. Since we defined id column as auto increment, we do not need to provide value for this column. It will be generated automatically. The date is in the format (yyyy-mm-dd). Note that any non-numerical values should be surrounded by quotes.

Using the phpMyAdmin Interface

Select 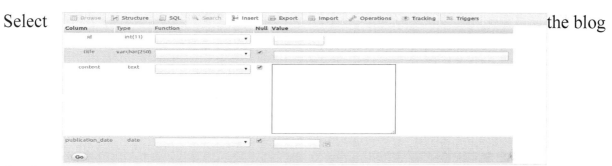 the blog database and then select article table. Then in the top navigation menu of phpMyAdmin, you will see an Insert option. If you click that option, you will see the following interface for inserting a new record into the article table -

As you can see, all the table columns are shown with input boxes to provide values. Leave the id column value empty and provide values for other columns and then click "Go" button to save the record to your table.

Retrieving Data from Table

The SELECT command is used for querying data from table. This is the command you will use a lot in your applications. The SELECT command can take a number of optional keywords. Let's start with the simple version of the SELECT command -

SELECT * FROM article;

This command simply says, 'select everything from the article table'. This will retrieve all the rows with all the columns from the table.

id	title	content	publication_date
1	test article	this is a test article	2014-03-01
2	another article	this is another article	2014-02-01
3	test article 2	this is another test article	2014-03-02
4	My article title goes here	this is article article content	2014-02-11

Let's say we only want the titles and content of the articles, in that case, we will use the following query -

SELECT title, content FROM article;

As you can see, instead of using the asterisk (*), we have specified only the title and content columns. As a result, we will get only the titles and contents of all the rows.

title	content
test article	this is a test article
another article	this is another article
test article 2	this is another test article
My article title goes here	this is article article content

Often we will want to selectively retrieve some of the rows instead of getting every row of a table. In that case, we use the WHERE keyword with our SELECT query -

SELECT * FROM article WHERE id=2;

This query will only retrieve the row with id value equals to 2. Since we have not specified any column but instead used the asterisk (*), all the columns of that row will be returned.

id	title	content	publication_date
2	another article	this is another article	2014-02-01

We can also use the WHERE condition to filter out results as well –

SELECT title, content FROM article WHERE title LIKE "%test%";

In this case, we have specified the title and content column and also used the WHERE condition to narrow down the number of rows retrieved. The WHERE condition contains the LIKE keyword which enables us to filter via pattern matching. In the above example, we have specified the pattern "%test%". What we have is the word "test" surrounded by percentage signs (%) on both side. This tells us to match any row with title containing the word "test". The percentage sign at the beginning indicates that, the word "test" can precede any sequence of characters, while the percentage sign after the word "test" indicates that, anything can follow the word "test". This way you can choose the pattern which best suits your purpose. The above query will return the following result -

title	content
test article	this is a test article
test article 2	this is another test article

In the WHERE clause, you can use comparison operators. The following query will retrieve articles with publication_date after "2014-02-28" -

SELECT * FROM article WHERE publication_date > "2014-02-28";

This will return the following result -

id	title	content	publication_date
1	test article	this is a test article	2014-03-01
3	test article 2	this is another test article	2014-03-02

Let's see another example of WHERE clause that uses the 'not equals to' operator -

*SELECT * FROM article WHERE id <> 3;*

This will return all the articles except the one with id equals to 3 -

id	title	content	publication_date
1	test article	this is a test article	2014-03-01
2	another article	this is another article	2014-02-01
4	My article title goes here	this is article content...	2014-02-11

You can also use more complex condition in your WHERE clause by combining multiple conditions using logical connectors like AND and OR. Let's have a look at the following example -

*SELECT * FROM article WHERE publication_date > "2014-02-05" AND title LIKE "%test%";*

This query will return all the articles that has a publication_date later than "2014-02-05" and also, that the article title contains the word "test" -

id	title	content	publication_date
1	test article	this is a test article	2014-03-01
3	test article 2	this is another test article	2014-03-02

Often your will need to sort the results of your query based on a particular column. The "ORDER BY" keyword can be used in the SELECT statement to sort the query results. With "ORDER BY", you can optionally use "ASC" for ascending or "DESC" for descending order. The default sort is ascending if you don't specify it -

SELECT * FROM article ORDER BY title DESC;

This will return all articles and order them by article title in descending order -

id	title ▾	content	publication_date
3	test article 2	this is another test article	2014-03-02
1	test article	this is a test article	2014-03-01
4	My article title goes here	this is article content...	2014-02-11
2	another article	this is another article	2014-02-01

Try populating your article table with a few sample articles and then run various select queries. That will help you understand databases better.

Updating Stored Data

We can update stored data using the UPDATE command. The general form of the UPDATE command looks like this -

UPDATE <tableName> SET
column1 = newValue1, ...
WHERE <conditions>;

Here 'column1' is the column name for which we want to update the value and 'newValue1' is the updated value of column1. If we need to update values for more than a single column, we separate the column-value pairs with comma (,) and then we set the WHERE condition to specify the row for which we want to update values. If we don't specify the WHERE condition, that will update values for all rows, so be cautious. Let's have a look at an example -

UPDATE article SET
title="New Title"
WHERE id=4;

This will update the row with id equals to 4 and will set the title column value to "New Title".

While updating rows, be sure to specify the WHERE condition to avoid updating other rows unintentionally.

Deleting Data from Table

You can delete data from your table using the DELETE command. The command has the following general form -

DELETE FROM <tableName> WHERE <condition>;

Again, use the WHERE condition to specify the row you want to delete. Let's delete a row from our article table -

DELETE FROM article WHERE id=4;

This will delete row with id equals to 4 from article table.

Summary

This chapter introduces us with MySQL. We have learned about how to create database, how to create tables and how to insert, update, delete and query data from our database. We have learned how to use the phpMyAdmin client to graphically perform database operations and also learned the SQL queries for performing different tasks. Those SQL commands will come in handy in the next chapter where we will use PHP to connect with a database and perform database operations to support our dynamic website.

Chapter 12: Using PHP and MySQL Together

In this chapter, we will learn how we can use PHP and MySQL together to build a database driven website. We will start with how we can connect a MySQL database from PHP. We will then learn how to execute MySQL queries from within our PHP scripts.

Connecting to MySQL Database

Before we can execute MySQL queries from our PHP scripts, first we need to connect to the database server. The mysqli_connect() function is used to connect to a MySQL database server. You need to provide the server name, database username and password as arguments to the mysqli_connect() function. Let's see how we can connect to our local MySQL database server with the user account "root" using an empty password -

```php
<?php
$server = "localhost";
$dbuser = "root";
$password = "";

$link = mysqli_connect($server, $dbuser, $password);
?>
```

The call to the mysqli_connect() function will open a database connection for your PHP script which will allow you to execute MySQL queries. This function returns a link identifier for the open database connection.

Selecting Database

Once you connect to a MySQL database using mysqli_connect() function, the next step should be to select a database. The mysqli_select_db() function is used to select a database. This function takes two parameters, first one is the link identifier return by mysqli_connect() function and the second parameter is the name of the database. Let's select our "blog" database that we have created in the previous chapter -

```php
<?php
$server = "localhost";
$dbuser = "root";
$password = "";
$link = mysqli_connect($server, $dbuser, $password);

mysqli_select_db($link, "blog");
?>
```

After you connect to your database server, you need to select your database using the mysqli_select_db() function.

Querying MySQL Database

In this section, we will see how we can execute MySQL queries from our PHP scripts. We will be using the same "article" table that we created in the previous chapter. Here is the SQL command for the article table -

```
CREATE TABLE article (
        id INT PRIMARY KEY AUTO_INCREMENT,
        title VARCHAR(250),
        content TEXT,
        publication_date DATE
);
```

Populate this "article" table with some entries. My "article" table is populated with the following entries -

id	title	content	publication_date
1	test article	this is a test article	2014-03-01
2	another article	this is another article	2014-02-01
3	test article 2	this is another test article	2014-03-02
4	My article title goes here	this is article content	2014-02-11

The mysqli_query() function is used to perform a query to the MySQL database.

158

You need to provide two parameters to this function, a link identifier returned by mysqli_connect() function and the query you want to perform.

Retrieving Data

Let's see how we can perform a SELECT query using the mysqli_query() function and then retrieve data from our "article" table.

```
<style>
    tr:nth-child(odd) {
        background-color:#e3e3e3;
    }

    tr:nth-child(even) {
        background-color:#ffffff;
    }

    tr:nth-child(1) {
        background-color: #6666FF;
    }
</style>

<?php
$server = "localhost";
$dbuser = "root";
$password = "";

$link = mysqli_connect($server, $dbuser, $password);
mysqli_select_db($link, "blog");

$sql = "SELECT * FROM article";
$result = mysqli_query($link, $sql);

echo "<table>";
echo "<tr>
            <td>Title</td>
            <td>Content</td>
            <td>Publication Date</td>
        </tr>";
while($row = mysqli_fetch_array($result)) {
```

159

```php
            $title = $row["title"];
            $content = $row["content"];
            $publication_date = $row["publication_date"];

            echo "<tr>
                    <td>$title</td>
                    <td>$content</td>
                    <td>$publication_date</td>
                </tr>";
}
echo "</table>";
mysqli_close($link);
?>
```

If we run this code, we will get the following output (given we have the "article" table populated with the data shown in the previous section) -

Title	Content	Publication Date
test article	this is a test article	2014-03-01
another article	this is another article	2014-02-01
test article 2	this is another test article	2014-03-02
My article title goes here	this is article content	2014-02-11

We will get a table of articles with title, content and publication date. Now let's go through the codes.

```css
<style>
    tr:nth-child(odd) {
        background-color:#e3e3e3;
    }

    tr:nth-child(even) {
        background-color:#ffffff;
    }

    tr:nth-child(1) {
        background-color: #6666FF;
    }
```

```
</style>
```

At the top of the file, we have a piece of CSS code to apply some style to our table to make it look nicer. We have selected odd and even rows and applied different background color to them. We have also set a different background color for the first row, which contains the table heading.

```
$sql = "SELECT * FROM article";
```

As you can see, we have assigned our SQL query to a variable named $sql. This query will simply select all the articles from our "article" table.

```
$result = mysqli_query($link, $sql);
```

We next use the mysqli_query() function to execute the SQL command assigned to the $sql variable. This function call will return the mysqli_result object. We assign this return value to $result variable.

```
echo "<table>";
echo "<tr>
        <td>Title</td>
        <td>Content</td>
        <td>Publication Date</td>
    </tr>";
```

This section of code outputs the code for a table with a single row and three columns. The row has the name of the columns: title, content and publication date. Other rows of the table will have these column values retrieved from the database and they will be generated dynamically with the below code.

```
while($row = mysqli_fetch_array($result)) {
    $title = $row["title"];
    $content = $row["content"];
    $publication_date = $row["publication_date"];

    echo "<tr>
            <td>$title</td>
            <td>$content</td>
            <td>$publication_date</td>
        </tr>";
}
```

In the above code, we have used a 'while' loop to iterate over the rows of the result returned by mysqli_query(). We have used mysqli_fetch_array() function, which takes the $result variable returned by mysqli_query() as argument and returned a result row as an array. With each iteration of the while loop, the mysqli_fetch_array() will return a result row of our query as an array. From the array, we can get the column values using the column names as index. In our above example, we have extracted three columns, title, content and publication_date.

```
echo "</table>";
```

This line outputs the closing </table> tag.

```
mysqli_close($link);
```

The mysqli_close() function will close the previously opened database connection.

The mysqli_fetch_array() function returns a result row of a query as an array. From that array, we can get the column values of the table using the column names as index.

Retrieve a Single Row from Table

In this section we will see how we can retrieve a single row from our 'article' table. Consider the scenario where your blog home page will contain summaries of some articles. Users will then have a 'read more' link to view the full article. Once you click that link, the article detailed page will be shown will full content, author, tags, category and son.

Let's build a simplified version of the blog home page that shows the titles of the article and a 'read more' link -

```
<style>
    tr:nth-child(even) {
        background-color:#33FF99;
    }

    tr:nth-child(odd) {
        background-color:#66CCFF;
```

```php
        }
</style>

<?php
$server = "localhost";
$dbuser = "root";
$password = "";

$link = mysqli_connect($server, $dbuser, $password);
mysqli_select_db($link, "blog");

$sql = "SELECT * FROM article";
$result = mysqli_query($link, $sql);

echo "<table>";
while($row = mysqli_fetch_array($result)) {
        $id = $row["id"];
        $title = $row["title"];

        echo "<tr>
                <td>$title</td>
                <td><a href='article_detail.php?id=$id'>Read More</a></td>
            </tr>";
}
echo "</table>";

mysqli_close($link);
?>
```

This will output the following result -

test article	Read More
another article	Read More
test article 2	Read More
My article title goes here	Read More

The code for the above script should look familiar to you. It's quite similar to the previous example. I have set in **bold** the changed portion of the code. In this case, we added a "Read More" link beside each article title.

<a href='article_detail.php?id=$id'>Read More</a>

As you can see, we have generated the URL for these hyper links dynamically using the article id obtained from the table. Now when someone clicks on the "Read More" link, this article id will be passed through the URL as a query string and we will be able to access that article id in the article_detail.php page. Then using that article id, we will retrieve the corresponding article from the table and show the details of that article. Let's examine the code for article_details.php page -

```php
<?php
$id = $_GET["id"];

$server = "localhost";
$dbuser = "root";
$password = "";

$link = mysqli_connect($server, $dbuser, $password);
mysqli_select_db($link, "blog");

$sql = "SELECT * FROM article WHERE id=$id";
$result = mysqli_query($link, $sql);

$row = mysqli_fetch_array($result);

$title = $row["title"];
$content = $row["content"];
$publication_date = $row["publication_date"];

mysqli_close($link);
?>

<h3><?php echo $title; ?></h3>
Published At: <?php echo $publication_date; ?>
<p><?php echo $content; ?></p>
```

Now if you click any "Read More" link, the article detail page will be shown as follows (assume we have clicked last link) -

SQL Injection

The previous section shows us how we can get article id from URL as query string and then execute a SQL query with this article id. While getting the user input and executing a SQL query with that user supplied value, you should be aware that malicious users can do bad things if you don't take security measures. Some users with bad intentions might execute a harmful SQL query and do big damage to your database. They can gain access to your website, change critical data inside database table or even empty your whole database table. This sort of attack by executing malicious SQL code is known as SQL injection. Let's consider an example, say you have a website with login form with username and password field -

From your PHP script, you will check this username and password using an SQL query like this (assuming someone has provided username "john" and password "mySecret")

*SELECT * FROM users WHERE username='john' AND password='mySecret';*

If there is any user registered with username "john" and password "mySecret" exists in your users table, then that user will gain access to your website.

Now let's see how a malicious user will bypass this authentication system using SQL injection. He will provide any arbitrary username (say "root") and for password, he will provide the value -

'OR 1=1--

Let's see what our SQL query looks like for this pair of username and password -

SELECT * FROM users WHERE username='root' AND password='' OR 1=1--;

This query will be true since the 1=1 is always true. This is how malicious users can gain access using SQL injection.

PHP provides a simple and elegant solution to handle this problem. All you have to do is to use mysql_real_escape_string() function to filter the input data -

```php
$username = mysql_real_escape_string($_POST["username"]);
$password = mysql_real_escape_string($_POST["password"]);
```

Use the mysql_real_escape_string() function for all your user input data to protect against SQL injection.

Closing the Database Connection

After you are done working with database related works from your PHP script, you need to close the active database connection. The mysqli_close() function will close the previously opened database connection. You can optionally provide the link identifier returned by mysqli_connection() function as argument to this mysqli_close() function to specifically tell the MySQL server to close that connection.

```php
<?php
mysqli_close($link);
?>
```

Once we have finished querying our database, we can close the active database connection using mysqli_close() function.

Inserting Data

Now let's see how we can insert data into our database from the PHP script. We can use mysqli_query() function for inserting data to the database. The mysqli_query() function will take the link identifier returned by mysqli_connect() function as the first argument and our second argument being the SQL command for inserting data -

```php
<?php
$server = "localhost";
$dbuser = "root";
$password = "";

$link = mysqli_connect($server, $dbuser, $password);
mysqli_select_db($link, "blog");

$sql = "INSERT INTO article (title, content, publication_date)
    VALUES('New article','this is a new article', '2014-03-04')";
mysqli_query($link, $sql);

mysqli_close($link);
?>
```

Running the above script will insert a new row to our "article" table with the specified data.

Example: Inserting Data into Database through Forms

In the previous section, we have learned how we can insert data into our database from a PHP script. In this section we will have a look at how we can insert data obtained from HTML forms, which is the most common method users interact with a website.

We will create a HTML form so that users of our website can contribute by submitting articles. Let's create the HTML form first -

```html
<p>Add New Article</p>

<form method="post" action="process.php">
    Title: <input type="text" name="title"/><br/>
    Content: <br/>
```

```html
        <textarea name="content" rows="10" cols="40"></textarea><br/>
        <input type="submit" name="submit" value="Add Article"/>
</form>
```

We have a simple HTML form with two input fields, one for article title and another for article content. Save the above code as form.php.

Once the form is submitted, the processing script of the form process.php is called. We create process.php to handle the submission of the above form. This process.php page will get form data using $_POST array. Then we will use these form data to construct our INSERT query and then execute that query using mysqli_query(). Here is the code for process.php page -

```php
<?php
$server = "localhost";
$dbuser = "root";
$password = "";

$link = mysqli_connect($server, $dbuser, $password);
mysqli_select_db($link, "blog");

$title = $_POST["title"];
$content = $_POST["content"];
$publication_date = date("Y-m-d");

$sql_insert = "INSERT INTO article (title, content, publication_date)
                        VALUES('$title','$content', '$publication_date')";

if(mysqli_query($link, $sql_insert)) {
      echo "Article added successfully!";
}
else {
      echo "An error occurred, try again!";
}

mysqli_close($link);
?>
```

Now let's put these two files under htdocs folder and run the form.php file from your browser. This is how it will look like -

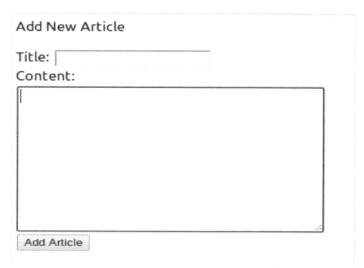

Add New Article

Title:

Content:

[Add Article]

If you fill the above form and then submit it, the process.php file will get the form data and insert a new article to our database.

Now let's examine the code of the above example -

```php
$title = $_POST["title"];
$content = $_POST["content"];
```

These two lines of code gets the title and content of the article from the form input. We access those data from the $_POST array and then store them to the $title and $content variables.

```php
$publication_date = date("Y-m-d");
```

In our HTML form, we don't have the 'publication date' field. Instead of getting the date as user input, we get the date dynamically using the PHP date() function.

```php
$sql_insert = "INSERT INTO article (title, content, publication_date)
                    VALUES('$title','$content', '$publication_date')";
```

This is the INSERT command for inserting new article to the database.

```php
if(mysqli_query($link, $sql_insert)) {
        echo "Article added successfully!";
}
else {
```

```
        echo "An error occurred, try again!";
}
```

Finally, we execute the SQL query for inserting a new article. We have used the if-else statement to check if the insert is successful or not. In summary, this is how we can use HTML form input data and then insert into our database.

Updating Data

You can easily update the rows of your database table in PHP. The same mysqli_query() function we have used earlier for querying and inserting data is also used for updating data. Let's see an example of executing a UPDATE query to update a row of our "article" table -

```
<?php
$server = "localhost";
$dbuser = "root";
$password = "";

$link = mysqli_connect($server, $dbuser, $password);
mysqli_select_db($link, "blog");

$sql = "UPDATE article SET title='Updated Title' WHERE id=3";
mysqli_query($link, $sql);

mysqli_close($link);
?>
```

The above script will update the title of the row with id equals to 3.

You can easily create an HTML form for updating existing data. This will be very similar to the insert form created in the previous section.

To provide our users a way to update articles, we typically provide a hyper link with the article id for editing the article. Once the user clicks that hyper link, we will show the edit form with form fields populated with existing data.

Now let's see how we can generate the "Edit Article" links, so that upon clicking on them, we can get the edit form populated with existing data -

170

```
<style>
    tr:nth-child(even) {
        background-color:#33FF99;
    }

    tr:nth-child(odd) {
        background-color:#66CCFF;
    }
</style>
<?php
$server = "localhost";
$dbuser = "root";
$password = "";

$link = mysqli_connect($server, $dbuser, $password);
mysqli_select_db($link, "blog");

$sql = "SELECT * FROM article";
$result = mysqli_query($link, $sql);

echo "<table>";
while($row = mysqli_fetch_array($result)) {
    $id = $row["id"];
    $title = $row["title"];

    echo "<tr>
            <td>$title</td>
            <td><a href='edit.php?id=$id'>Edit Article</a></td>
        </tr>";
}
echo "</table>";

mysqli_close($link);
?>
```

This will output -

test article	Edit Article
another article	Edit Article
test article 2	Edit Article
My article title goes here	Edit Article

The above code should be familiar to you. The bolded line provides links to edit articles. We are passing the article id as query string, so once the user clicks on that article link, we will be able to access the article id from the edit.php page. Now let's see the code for edit.php -

```php
<?php
$server = "localhost";
$dbuser = "root";
$password = "";

$id = mysql_real_escape_string($_GET["id"]);

$link = mysqli_connect($server, $dbuser, $password);
mysqli_select_db($link, "blog");

$sql = "SELECT * FROM article WHERE id=$id";
$result = mysqli_query($link, $sql);

$row = mysqli_fetch_array($result);

$title = $row["title"];
$content = $row["content"];

mysqli_close($link);
?>

<p>Edit Article</p>

<form method="post" action="process.php">
    <input type="hidden" name="id" id="<?php echo $id; ?>"/>
    Title: <input type="text" name"title" value="<?php echo $title; ?>"/><br/>
    Content: <br/>
```

172

```
        <textarea name="content" rows="10" cols="40"><?php echo $content; ?></
textarea><br/>
        <input type="submit" name="submit" value="Update Article"/>
</form>
```

This will show an edit form with form fields populated with previous data (see below) -

We are passing the article id as a hidden form field. Now the corresponding form handling page (process.php) should contain the SQL query for updating the article with the new form data. Let's see the code for process.php file -

```
<?php
$server = "localhost";
$dbuser = "root";
$password = "";

$link = mysqli_connect($server, $dbuser, $password);
mysqli_select_db($link, "blog");

$id = mysql_real_escape_string($_POST['id']);
$title = mysql_real_escape_string($_POST['title']);
$content = mysql_real_escape_string($_POST['content']);
```

```php
$sql = "UPDATE article SET title='$title', content='$content' WHERE id=$id";
mysqli_query($link, $sql);
echo "Article updated successfully!";

mysqli_close($link);
?>
```

Once the user updates the article and submits the form using "Update Article" button, this process.php script will be called and the corresponding article will be updated in your database.

Deleting Data

Finally let's see how to delete a row from the database table. There is nothing special about executing the DELETE command from PHP. We will again use the mysqli_query() function and the logic will be very similar to the updating data as explained earlier.

Typically your website will have a bunch of delete article links, which will have hyper links with the article id, once you will click that delete article link, the article id will be passed as query string and you will execute DELETE command with that article id -

```html
<style>
    tr:nth-child(even) {
        background-color:#33FF99;
    }

    tr:nth-child(odd) {
        background-color:#66CCFF;
    }
</style>

<?php
$server = "localhost";
$dbuser = "root";
$password = "";

$link = mysqli_connect($server, $dbuser, $password);
```

```php
mysqli_select_db($link, "blog");

$sql = "SELECT * FROM article";
$result = mysqli_query($link, $sql);

echo "<table>";
while($row = mysqli_fetch_array($result)) {
    $id = $row["id"];
    $title = $row["title"];

    echo "<tr>
            <td>$title</td>
            <td><a href='delete.php?id=$id'>Delete Article</a></td>
        </tr>";
}
echo "</table>";

mysqli_close($link);
?>
```

Take a look at the bolded line. With it, we have created hyper links to the delete.php page with article id passed as query string. This page will look like below-

test article	Delete Article
another article	Delete Article
test article 2	Delete Article
My article title goes here	Delete Article

Once you click the "Delete Article" link, the delete.php page will be called. Let's see the code for delete.php page -

```php
<?php
$server = "localhost";
$dbuser = "root";
$password = "";
```

```php
$id = mysql_real_escape_string($_GET["id"]);

$link = mysqli_connect($server, $dbuser, $password);
mysqli_select_db($link, "blog");

$sql = "DELETE FROM article WHERE id='$id'";
mysqli_query($link, $sql);
echo "Article deleted successfully!"
mysqli_close($link);
?>
```

This delete.php page will get article id using $_GET array and then we will execute the delete command. As a result, the article will be removed from database.

Summary

We have learned about how to connect to a MySQL database from our PHP scripts and execute SQL queries. In the next chapter, we will learn about sessions and cookies.

Chapter 13: Cookies and Sessions

In this chapter we will learn about Cookies and Sessions. The built in functions provided by PHP made it easy to handle both cookies and sessions, but first we will understand the basic concepts behind them. We will learn what cookies and sessions are, why we need to use them in our web applications and then finally how we can use them in our websites easily.

HTTP – The Stateless Protocol

The Hyper Text Transfer Protocol (HTTP) is the protocol for data communication of the world wide web which is a stateless protocol. You might ask what is a stateless protocol? When you request a web page using a web browser and the web server sends back the response which is interpreted by your web browser, the connection between your web browser and server is closed. Subsequent requests sent by your web browser to the same web server do not have any clue about the previous request. This is the stateless nature of the HTTP protocol. The problem with this is that it will not allow you to create any user centric applications at all. To overcome this problem, cookies were introduced and later on, sessions.

HTTP is a stateless protocol. After the web server responds to the current request, it has no information about subsequent requests.

Cookies

Cookies are tiny bits of data stored by a website in a client's computer. The idea behind cookies are, when a user first visits a website, the website will send tiny bits of information to the browser. This information will be stored in the user's machine. Later when the user visits that particular website again, the browser will send those stored information back to the website with the HTTP request. The web server will retrieve those information and with it, be able to identify the user.

A cookie is actually a name-value pair, which is associated with the particular website that sets the cookie. Only that corresponding website can access the cookie, other websites will not be able to access that. Now let's see how we can use cookies in PHP scripts.

177

Cookies are tiny bits of information stored by a website on to a client's computer. The stored information is later retrieved by that website on subsequent requests.

Setting Up Cookies

The setcookie() function is used for setting a cookie. You need to provide three parameters to this setcookie() function, name of the cookie, the value of the cookie and expire time of the cookie. The following example sets a cookie with name "myCookie", which will expire in one hour -

```php
<?php
$val = "some value here";

setcookie("myCookie", $val, time()+3600);

?>
```

The expire time is set as

```
time() + 3600;
```

The time() function returns the current timestamp, and we add 3600 seconds to that value which will give us expiration time of one hour.

Accessing Cookies

You can access the values of the cookies by using the array $_COOKIE. Lets see how we can access the cookie named "myCookie" set earlier -

```php
<?php
echo $_COOKIE["myCookie"];
?>
```

If you want to delete a cookie that has expiry time set in future, you can delete it by changing the expiry time to represent any past time. The following example shows how we can delete a cookie explicitly be setting the expiry time to past -

```php
<?php
```

```php
setcookie("myCookie", $val, time()-3600);
?>
```

Example: Visitor Counter

Now we will have a look at an example that demonstrates the usage of Cookies. We will build a simple visitor counter, which will show the user how many times they have visited the web page.

```php
<?php

//if this is the first time visit, initialize $total_visits to 0
if(!isset($_COOKIE["visit_count"])) {
      $total_visits = 0;
}
//otherwise get the count of previous visits from COOKIE
else {
      $total_visits = $_COOKIE["visit_count"];
}

//increse $total_visits by 1
$total_visits += 1;

//set the cookie "visit_count" with new $total_visits, with expiration time for 365 days
setcookie("visit_count", $total_visits, time() + 3600*24*365);

echo "You have visited: $total_visits time(s).";
?>
```

Save this PHP script to your local server and run from your browser, for your first visit, you will get the following output -

> You have visited: 1 time(s).

Then with your subsequent visit to this page, you will see the visit count increase.

Now let me explain how the script is working. First we check if the cookie named "visit_count" is already set. We have used isset() function to check that. The isset() function will return true if the variable passed as it's argument is set.

We use a variable named $total_visits to hold the value of previous visits. So, in case the cookie "visit_count" isn't set, then we initialize the variable $total_visits and set it's value to 0, otherwise we get the value of previous visits count from $_COOKIE array and set that to $total_visits.

Then we increase the value of $total_visits to take into account the current visit and set the cookie "visit_count" with new value of $total_visits. You can see that for subsequent visits, the previous visit counts are retrieved from the cookie and that cookie is reset by increasing the value by one. This is how we get the updated visit count every time.

While using cookies, you need to be aware that browsers limit the number of cookies allowed per site. This is browser specific and therefore there is no single rule, but some browsers allow 20 cookies per website. Beyond that limit, old cookies might be deleted for that website. So instead of overusing the cookies, try to keep the usage within limit.

Another thing to consider is the fact that, users have the option to disable cookie from browsers settings. In that case, the browser will not accept cookies from your website. One last thing I would like to mention is the security concern. Cookies are saved to user's computer, so if the user is intelligent enough and possess the adequate knowledge, he can temper the data saved as cookies. So you shouldn't store any secure data like passwords or credit card numbers as cookies.

Sessions

Sessions actually evolved from cookies. In the case of sessions, as opposed to storing data on the client's machine, the session data is stored in the server. For that reason, the session data is more secure because users don't have access to those data and can't temper them. In addition to that, because session data is stored on server side, it is possible to store more data in contrast to cookie data which are limited by browser restrictions. Sessions may still use a small cookie to hold the session identifier. The job of this cookie which holds the session identifier is to identify the user and reference the correct data stored in the server.

Session data are stored on servers with a small cookie used to hold the session identifier.

Starting a Session

Before using a session, you need to call the session_start() function, which will start the session. The session_start() function checks whether a visitor sent a session cookie. If this is the case, PHP will load session data from the server. Else, a new session file will be created on the server and a cookie will be sent with session identifier to the browser.

```php
<?php
session_start();
?>
```

Call the session_start() function before you output any content to the browser, otherwise you will see an error. Typically, you place the session_start() call at the beginning of your PHP file.

You start a session by calling the session_start() function.

Working with Session Data

The $_SESSION array is used to work with session data. You can add and access session data using this $_SESSION array. Let's see how we can add a new session data -

```php
<?php
//add a new session data
$_SESSION["name"] = "John";
?>
```

Accessing session data is also simple -

```php
<?php
//accessing session data
$name = $_SESSION["name"];
?>
```

Let's see an example that uses session. First, create a page called hello.php with the following code -

```php
<?php
session_start();

if(isset($_SESSION["name"])) {
        echo "Hello ".$_SESSION["name"];
}
else {
        echo "Welcome Guest";
}
?>


<form action="process.php" method="post">
        Name:<input type="text" name="name"/>
        <input type="submit" name="submit" value="Set Name"/>
</form>
```

The script will check if a session called "name" is set. If it is true, a message with user's name will be shown, otherwise a generic message will be shown. There is also a HTML form with a text field, which allows the user to set their name. When a user submits that form, the processing script of the form "process.php" will be called. Let's see the code for process.php file -

```php
<?php
session_start();

$name = $_POST["name"];

$_SESSION["name"] = $name;
?>


<p>Name Set Successfully.</p>
<a href="hello.php">Click here</a> to go to previous page.
```

Here we get the user's input using $_POST array, which is the name user has set. We then save this name to the $_SESSION array. Next, save both the hello.php and process.php file under the same directory of your local web server (htdocs folder) and run the hello.php file (http://localhost/hello.php) -

182

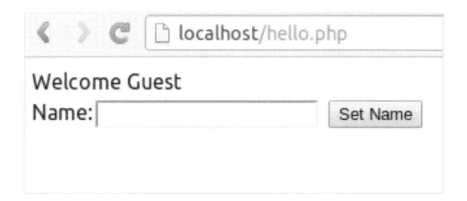

Since the session "name" isn't set yet, we will see a generic greeting message. Now say we set our name as "Robert" and click the "Set Name" button -

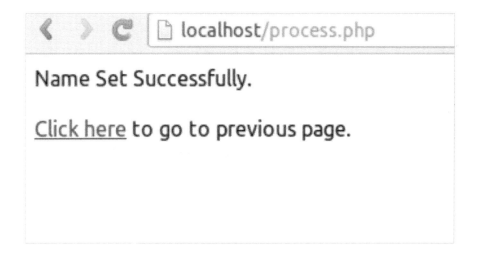

We will see the above message. Now if we click the link to go back to previous page, we will see following output -

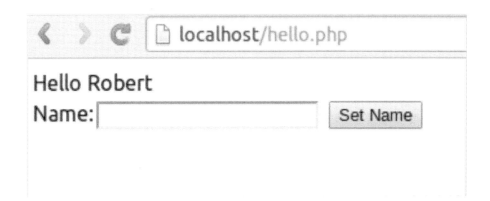

Now in our hello.php page, we are getting a greeting message with the name set earlier, because that name is saved as session data in process.php page.

Removing Session Data

You can remove session data using the unset() function call -

```php
<?php
session_start();
unset($_SESSION["name"]);
?>
```

This will remove the session called "name".

If you wish to delete all session data, then you can call session_destroy() function, which will destroy the entire session data -

```php
<?php
session_start();
session_destroy();
?>
```

session_destroy() will end your current session and destroy all session data.

Summary

We have learned about the statelessness nature of HTTP and the techniques to overcome this problem: cookies and sessions. Using them carefully, we can build applications that keeps the state of browsing between multiple sessions. The next chapter will show us how we can do file uploads using PHP.

Chapter 14: Handling File Uploads

In this chapter, we will learn how we can upload files with PHP. Uploading of files is a common task in many websites. For example - if you have a forum website, users might want to upload their profile pictures or photos of products to sell online. In either case, the capability to upload files from your website is essential.

Uploading Files with PHP

The HTML form <input> tag with **type** attribute set to "file" enables us to provide an input area for uploading files. You can include this input element to your HTML form the same way you include other input elements. This "file" input element will be shown as a "browse" or "select" button when viewed from web browsers. One other thing you need to take care of in your HTML form is that you need to add an attribute called "enctype" of "multipart/form-data" to the <form> tag. Let's see the example below -

```
<form method="post" action="process.php" enctype="multipart/form-data">
File:<input type="file" name="myfile"/><br/>
<input type="submit"/>
</form>
```

Save this file as file_upload.php and this is how it will look like -

You can see a "Choose File" option, which will let the user choose file from file directory for uploading. This file upload form is just one part of the process of uploading file. The receiving and subsequent handling of the uploaded file will be done server side using PHP. Let's see the code of process.php file -

```
<?php
echo "Uploaded File Information:<br/>";
echo "File Name: ".$_FILES["myfile"]["name"]."<br/>";
echo "File Size: ".$_FILES["myfile"]["size"]."<br/>";
```

```
echo "File Type: ".$_FILES["myfile"]["type"];
?>
```

Now say we upload an image file "my_avatar.png", the process.php file will give following output -

Uploaded File Information:
File Name: my_avatar.png
File Size: 227514
File Type: image/png

We will see the information of the uploaded file, like file name, file size in bytes and type of the file.

The $_FILES Array

The $_FILES array contains the information about the uploaded file. We access these information using the 'name' attribute of the file input tag specified in HTML form. The example shown in the above section has the name attribute of value "myfile", so we can access the information of the uploaded file using $_FILES["myfile"].

$_FILES["myfile"] itself is an array. This array has file indexes, which provides useful information regarding the file upload attempt -

- $_FILES["myfile"]["name"] - This will return the original name of the uploaded file with file extension.

- $_FILES["myfile"]["size"] - We will get the file's size in bytes by accessing this index.

- $_FILES["myfile"]["type"] - This specifies the MIME type of the uploaded file.

- $_FILES["myfile"]["tmp_name"] - This variable specifies the temporary location of the file once it has been uploaded to the server.

186

- $_FILES["myfile"]["error"] - This value offers important information regarding the outcome of file upload attempt. In case of successful file upload, this will return a value of 0.

The $_FILES array contains information about the uploaded image.

Moving an Uploaded File

The file after being uploaded is stored in a temporary directory on the server. After you upload your file, you should move this file to a more convenient location. The move_uploaded_file() function is used to move a uploaded file from temporary directory to your storage place. This function takes two parameters, first parameter is the temporary location of the uploaded file and second parameter is the new location. Let's see how we can use this function -

```php
<?php
move_uploaded_file($_FILES["myfile"]["tmp_name"],
                                "uploads/".$_FILES["myfile"]["name"]);
?>
```

Here we have specified the "uploads" sub-directory, which is located under the same directory of the PHP script to store the uploaded file. We can also provide the full path of "uploads" directory using the getcwd() function -

```php
<?php
move_uploaded_file($_FILES["myfile"]["tmp_name"],
                                getcwd()."/uploads/".$_FILES["myfile"]
["name"]);
?>
```

The getcwd() function returns the current working directory, which is the directory under which the currently executing PHP script is stored. So by appending the getcwd() function to the "uploads" directory's path, we get the full path of the "uploads" directory.

The move_uploaded_file() also checks if the specified file is uploaded. If the file upload is failed, then this function will return false, otherwise it returns true. So you can check the return value of the move_uploaded_file() function to make sure file is uploaded or not as well.

The move_uploaded_file() function checks if the file is uploaded and also moves the uploaded file from the temporary location to a user-specified directory.

Example: Image Upload Script

We will see next how to write a simple image upload script, which will only allow users to upload JPG or PNG images. We will also move the image from a temporary location to a permanent directory. First, let's create the form -

```
<form method="post" action="process_upload.php" enctype="multipart/form-data">
Select Image File: (JPG or PNG format)<br/>
<input type="file" name="img_file"/><br/>
<input type="submit" value="Upload!"/>
</form>
```

Save this file as image_upload.php and run it from the browser. It will look as follows -

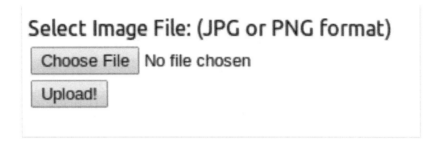

Now let's see the code for process_upload.php file -

```php
<?php

if($_FILES["img_file"]["type"] == "image/jpeg" ||
  $_FILES["img_file"]["type"] == "image/jpg" ||
  $_FILES["img_file"]["type"] == "image/png") {

    if(move_uploaded_file($_FILES["img_file"]["tmp_name"],
      "uploads/".$_FILES["img_file"]["name"])) {
        echo "Image uploaded successfully!";
    }
    else {
```

```
        echo "Error processing uploaded image!";
    }
}
else {
    echo "You must choose either JPG or PNG file!";
}

?>
```

The outer if-else conditional is checking the uploaded file's format. If the uploaded file is of type jpg or png, we will then move the uploaded file. Otherwise we show an error message to the user.

Summary

We have learned how to upload files using PHP. As we have seen in the above section, PHP enables us to upload files with ease & convenience. In the next chapter, we will discuss about some security concerns related to web development and how we can protect our websites from malicious users. We will also learn some good practices to make our code more readable and manageable. make our code more readable and manageable.

Chapter 15: Security Concerns and Good Practices

In this chapter, we will learn about some security concerns that you should be aware of while developing your web applications. We will also have a look at some of the good practices you should follow at the end of this chapter.

Security

You web site is intended to be accessible by people all over the world, but not all of them have a friendly attitude though. There are some bad guys who are seeking to exploit your web application. That is why you should take the necessary security precautions to make your web application secure and less vulnerable to attacks from these bad guys. The following sections will list some of the security measures you can adopt in developing a secure web application.

Do Not Store Password as Plain Text

Any website with user login capability needs to store username and password in database. These credentials are used to verify user authenticity. Now, you shouldn't store passwords as plain text. Instead, use the hashing function to encrypt the password and then store that the hashed password in your database. PHP provides many hashing functions like md5(), sha1(). Take a look at the following code snippet, which produces a hash string using the sha1() function -

```php
<?php
$password = "mySecret";
$hash_str = sha1($password);
?>
```

This is how you produce the hash string of a password. You will store this hash string instead of the plain text password.

Note that this hashing is a one way process. You cannot decrypt the hashed string to get back the original text. So when you want to authenticate any user, you will need to compare the password entered by them against the stored password. In that case, you will produce the hash string of the password that user has entered while attempting to login and compare that hash string with the stored hash string in your database.

If you stored the hash string of passwords, even if someone gets access to your database, they will not be able to retrieve your password as plain text. Instead they will get the hashed string of your password and thus unable to login with your account.

You should encrypt a password store its hashed string before storing them in a database.

Do Not Put Any Sensitive Data in Cookies

As mentioned earlier, Cookies are stored in the client's machine. Users have control over those cookie files. If the user possesses the right knowledge, he can temper the cookie data the way he wants. That's why you should be careful about what you are going to store as cookie data. You should never store any potentially secure data like password or credit card information as cookie data. Instead use secure storage like database for this purpose.

Do Not Trust User Input

You should never ever trust user input. Some users can be malicious and they can perform potentially dangerous tasks for your website. While some users might make a mistake and provide values in wrong formats, it is the programmer's job to make sure that your web application can handle user input properly, notifies users in case incorrect values are provided and also filter the input data to protect the users from malicious activities.

The filter_var() function comes in handy for the purpose of filtering user inputs. This function takes two parameters. The first parameter is the data you want to filter and the second parameter is the filter you want to apply to that data. Let's see an example on how we can check if the user provides an email address in correct format using the filter_var() function -

```php
<?php
$email = "user@example.com";

if(filter_var($email, FILTER_VALIDATE_EMAIL)) {
```

```
        //valid email, do some task here
}
?>
```

Note that there are other filters available. Take a look at the official PHP documentation for all other available filters -

http://www.php.net/manual/en/filter.filters.validate.php

Similarly you should filter user inputs before using the raw SQL query. Use the mysql_real_excape_string() function to filter all user inputs as this will protect you against an SQL injection attack (we have discussed SQL injection attack in chapter 12).

User submitted values should be filtered and validated before working with them.

Good Practices

The following sections will discuss some of the good practices you should follow while programming in PHP.

Use Meaningful Variable Names

While using variables in your program, you should try to use meaningful names for them. Using generic variable names like $foo, $bar should be avoided because they do not convey any information about the value stored in the variable. Similarly you should avoid using short variable names like $x, $y (with exception to using them as temporary variables, like as for loop counter). Let's see an example of using meaningful variable names -

```
<?php
$x = 4;
$y = 3.14 * pow($x,2);
?>
```

After having a quick look at the above program, not all of you will immediately understand what the variables $x and $y are used for. However, if we name those variables as follows, it would make more sense to us -

192

```php
<?php
$radius = 4;
$area = 3.14 * pow($radius,2);
?>
```

Now someone looking at the above code will have a better idea about the values of the variables.

Indent Your Code Properly

Format your code by using code indentation. Code residing at the same level should have the same indentation. For example, indent the lines of code which are within loop or conditionals. That will make your code more readable.

Let's look at an example -

```php
<?php
$counter = 0;
while ($counter < 10) {
echo $counter;
$counter++;
}
?>
```

The above code is badly indented, instead we could have done something like this -

```php
<?php
$counter = 0;
while ($counter < 10) {
    echo $counter;
    $counter++;
}
?>
```

With this, someone can examine the code inside the while loop more easily. Once your program grows in complexity, indentations will make your code much more navigable.

Comment Your Code

Make use of comments within your code. It will be invaluable when someone else will attempts to understand your code, or even helpful to yourself when you look at your code few months (or years) later. For any portion of code whose usage doesn't seem obvious, use comments to make a note of the logic behind that portion of code.

Following Coding Standards

Over time, various coding standards have evolved among the PHP developers community. You should adopt a standard to make your code more readable to other developers. Below are the links of few of the coding standards you can follow -

Pear Coding Standards
http://pear.php.net/manual/en/standards.php

Zend Coding Standards
http://framework.zend.com/wiki/display/ZFDEV2/Coding+Standards

Symfony Coding Standards
http://symfony.com/doc/current/contributing/code/standards.html

It is important to note that whatever coding standard you follow, you should be consistent to apply it throughout your project.

Where Next?

By now you should be quite proficient at working with PHP. Work on different projects to give you a 'hands on' experience of web development with PHP. There are other advanced features of PHP we haven't explored in this book, but you have the foundation which will allow you to learn more about PHP from other resources. There are thousands of excellent resources available online for you, many of them are completely free. Below is a list of just few of the resources you can follow -

Official PHP Documentation

The official PHP documentation, available at http://php.net/ is an excellent place to learn more about PHP. In addition to official documentation, this website has a lots of examples and comments contributed by other PHP developers.

Tuts+ PHP Tutorials

Tuts+ has a huge collection of excellent PHP tutorials, you can find these at -

http://code.tutsplus.com/categories/php

DreamInCode PHP Tutorials

The popular programming community dreamInCode.net has lots of PHP tutorials and code snippets.

Tutorials - http://www.dreamincode.net/forums/showforum47.htm
Code Snippets - http://www.dreamincode.net/forums/forum/213-php-snippets/

Advanced PHP Books

You can pick an advanced PHP book, lots of good PHP books out there. Some of the good titles are -

Beginning PHP and MySQL From Novice to Professional – By W Jason Gilmore
http://www.apress.com/9781430231141

PHP5 Power Programming – By Andi Gutmans, Stig Bakken and Derick Rethans
http://www.amazon.com/PHP-Power-Programming-Andi-Gutmans/dp/013147149X

PHP Objects, Patters and Practice – By Matt Zandstra
https://www.apress.com/9781430229254

Example Project – Building a Simple E-commerce Website

We have learned the basic concepts needed for web development. In this example project, we will see how we can create a simple e-commerce website using the techniques we have learned. With this example, we hope that it will give you an idea on how the different concepts learned fit together to develop your own dynamic website.

Planning the Work Flow

Before we start writing codes for our website, we need to do some planning. We need to have a guideline of the steps we will be taking. Our work flow will roughly consists of -

- We will begin by defining our project outline. By that I mean that we will need to understand what we are going to build and what will be the features of our website.
- If the project consists of storing data, we will need to think about the database design and then create database tables for it.
- Finally, we start building PHP pages for our website.

Project Outline

We will be building a simplified version of an e-commerce website. Building a fully functional e-commerce web application is a complex process. In this example, we will just build a basic version of an e-commerce web application but yet cover the essential fundamental building blocks for you to go on and build your own complex website. We will build both the frontend and backend of the website.

The frontend will have -

- A product catalog through which users browse through available products
- A shopping cart where users add products for checkout
- The checkout page which will show the contents of the user's shopping cart for confirmation

The backend of the website will have -
- A product insertion page, through which we add new products to our website
- A product management panel with the option to update or remove existing product
- An update product page where we update information of an existing product
- The delete product functionality

Database Design

A fully featured e-commerce site will have a number of database tables, including a table for storing user information, product information, purchase information etc. However in our simplified version of the e-commerce website to make your learning easier, we will only store product information in our database. We will only need one table, which we will call "products". Our products table will have the following fields -
- product_id – primary key of the table, will be of type INT
- product_name – will contain the product name, will be of type VARCHAR
- product_description – this will contain a short description of our product, will be of type TEXT
- product_price – the price of the product, will be of type FLOAT
- product_image – to store the product image file name

Creating the Database

Before we can create the products table, we will need to create a database (or select an existing database). We will create a new database called "e-commerce".

We will create the e-commerce database from phpMyAdmin. Visit -http://localhost/phpmyadmin/ from your browser and login with your database username and password. Next, from the top navigation bar, select "Databases" option -

From the next screen, create the "e-commerce" database -

Alternatively, you can create the "e-commerce" database using the following SQL command -

CREATE DATABASE e-commerce;

You can execute this SQL command by selecting the "SQL" tab from top navigation option of phpMyAdmin -

Creating the "products" Table

Now select the "e-commerce" database (which you have created in the previous step) from the left sidebar of phpMyAdmin -

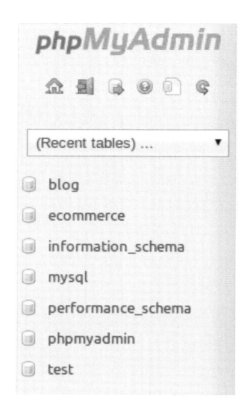

Next, execute the following SQL command to create "products" table -

```
CREATE TABLE products (
    product_id INT PRIMARY KEY AUTO_INCREMENT,
    product_name VARCHAR(200),
    product_description TEXT,
    product_price DOUBLE(11,2),
    product_image VARCHAR(200)
);
```

Now that we have created our database and table, let's move on to create the pages of our website.

Website Project Structure

When building a website, we should keep our files organized. We will put all the files of our e-commerce website under the directory "e-commerce". So let's create a new directory named "e-commerce" under the root directory of our local web server (htdocs folder). Our e-commerce website will have both frontend and backend files. We will put all the frontend files under the "e-commerce" directory, but will create another directory for putting the backend files calling it the "admin" directory.

Image files will be stored under the "images" directory. CSS files for the frontend of the website will be stored separately in a directory named "css" under the main project directory (under "e-commerce" directory). We will create another "css" directory under "e-commerce/admin" directory which will hold the CSS files for admin portion of the website. In all, the project structure will look something like this -

```
htdocs/
|---ecommerce/
|       |---frontend php files
|       |---css/
|       |       |---frontend css files
|       |---images/
|       |       |---image files
|       |---admin/
|       |       |---admin php files
|       |       |---css/
|       |       |       |---admin css files
```

Backend Development

We will start with creating the backend portion of the website. All the files of our backend will be placed under the "htdocs/e-commerce/admin" directory.

Product Insert Page

First we will create a page for users to add new products. We create a new page, called "add_product.php" under the "e-commerce/admin" directory, which will have contain a form to add new product information.

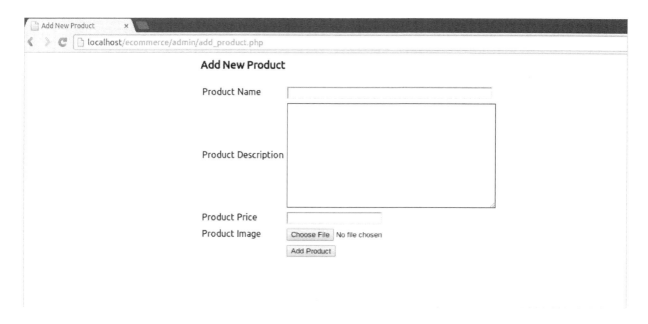

Now let's look at the code for the add_product.php page -

```html
<html>
<head>
    <title>Add New Product</title>
    <link rel="stylesheet" type="text/css" href="css/style.css"/>
</head>

<body>
    <div id="content">
        <h3>Add New Product</h3>
        <form method="post" action="process_insert.php"

    enctype="multipart/form-data">
        <table>
            <tr>
                <td>Product Name</td>
                <td><input type="text" name="product_name"
size="45"/></td>
            </tr>
            <tr>
                <td>Product Description</td>
                <td><textarea name="product_description" rows="10"
cols="45"></textarea></td>
            </tr>
            <tr>
```

```
                    <td>Product Price</td>
                    <td><input type="text" name="product_price"/></td>
              </tr>
              <tr>

                    <td>Product Image</td>
                    <td><input type="file" name="product_image"/> </td>
              </tr>
              <tr>

                    <td>andnbsp;</td>
                    <td><input type="submit" value="Add Product"/></td>
              </tr>
          </table>
          </form>
      </div>
</body>
</html>
```

This file has a reference to a style sheet. Let's create the "style.css" file under the directory "e-commerce/admin/css" -

```
#content {
      width: 650px;
      margin:0 auto;
}
```

This CSS file has a single rule, which sets the width of the div named "content" to 650px and set margin property of "0 auto" which applies 0 margin to top and bottom of the div. It will also apply margin "auto" to left and right of that div. The margin with value "auto" will split the available margin equally and leave them to both sides of the div.

Now let's see the code for process_insert.php page which will handle the form submission of the above page -

```
<?php
require_once("db.connect.php");

$product_name = mysql_real_escape_string($_POST["product_name"]);
$product_description =
mysql_real_escape_string($_POST["product_description"]);
```

```php
$product_price = mysql_real_escape_string($_POST["product_price"]);
$product_image = $_FILES["product_image"]["name"];

//move the uploaded image to images directory
move_uploaded_file($_FILES["product_image"]["tmp_name"],
                   "../images/".$_FILES["product_image"]["name"]);

$sql = "INSERT INTO products (product_name, product_description,
product_price,                    product_image)
        VALUES('$product_name', '$product_description',
                               '$product_price',
'$product_image')";
?>
<html>
<head>
    <title>Add Product</title>
    <link rel="stylesheet" type="text/css" href="css/style.css"/>
</head>
<body>
    <div id="content">
    <?php
        if(mysqli_query($link, $sql)) {
            echo "<p>Product Added Successfully!</p>";
        }
        else {
            echo mysqli_error($link);
        }
    ?>
    <p><a href="add_product.php">Add Another Product</a></p>
    </div>
</body>
</html>
```

Once you insert a new product and submit the form, it will take you to the process_insert.php page and show the following output -

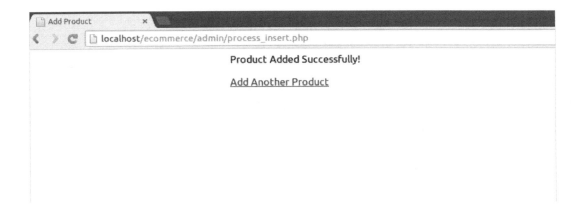

Now let's go through the code of the "process_insert.php" file -

require_once("db.connect.php");

This includes the contents of "db.connect.php" file which has the code for database connection. If it doesn't find the "db.connect.php" file, the execution of the current script will be halted. Instead of putting the database connection information within the "process_insert.php" file, we have chosen to put this information in a separate file since we will need to connect to database from other files as well. By putting these information within "db.connect.php" file, we can simply include that within other files easily.

Below is the content of "db.connect.php" file, create this file under the directory "e-commerce/admin" with the following content -

```php
<?php
$server = "localhost";
$dbuser = "root";
$dbpass = "";
$dbname = "e-commerce";

$link = mysqli_connect($server, $dbuser, $dbpass);

mysqli_select_db($link, $dbname);
?>
```

Now you understand how to insert a piece of code from another file using require_once() function. The rest of the codes of process_insert.php file should look familiar to you. We get data using $_POST array and then use mysql_real_escape_string() function to escape those user input values.

```
$product_image = $_FILES["product_image"]["name"];
```

This line of code gives us the image file name. We will not store the actual image within the database. Rather, we just store the image file name. The actual image will be stored within the file system of the server.

```
//move the uploaded image to images directory
move_uploaded_file($_FILES["product_image"]["tmp_name"],
           "../images/".$_FILES["product_image"]["name"]);
```

This piece of code moves the uploaded image to the images directory which is under "e-commerce" directory.

We next construct the INSERT query and store it in $sql variable. Finally, we execute the query using mysqli_query() function and use a if-else statement to make sure if the query is successful or not -

```
if(mysqli_query($link, $sql)) {
     echo "<p>Product Added Successfully!</p>";
}
else {
     echo mysqli_error($link);
}
```

In the case when the query is successful, we show a message to the user. Else, we use the mysqli_error() function to get the information about whatever error has occurred.

Product Management Page

Next, we will create a page to manage the products already added to our database. This page will have the option to edit or delete products in our "products" table -

Let's create a new page, called "index.php" under the "e-commerce/admin" directory. We want this product management page to be the default page of our admin section. Put the below codes in your index.php page -

```php
<?php
require_once("db.connect.php");
?>

<html>
<head>
    <title>Manage Products</title>
    <link rel="stylesheet" type="text/css" href="css/style.css"/>
</head>
<body>
    <?php
    $sql = "SELECT product_id,product_name FROM products";

    $result = mysqli_query($link, $sql);

    $products = array();

    while($row = mysqli_fetch_array($result)) {
        $products[] = $row;
    }
    mysqli_close($link);
    ?>

    <div id="content">
        <h3>Manage Products</h3>
        <a href="add_product.php">Add New Product</a>
```

```
<table class="products_table">
        <?php foreach($products as $product): ?>
        <tr>
                <td><?php echo $product["product_name"];?></td>
                <td><a href="edit.php?id=<?php echo

$product["product_id"]; ?>">Edit</a></td>
                <td><a href="delete.php?id=<?php echo

$product["product_id"]; ?>">Delete</a></td>
        </tr>
        <?php endforeach; ?>
    </table>
</div>

</body>
</html>
```

Since this index.php page will need to interact with database to retrieve existing products, we include the database connection code as usual -

```
require_once("db.connect.php");
```

When we have retrieved all the products from our "products" table and stored them in $products array, we will use $products array later to show the products.

```
<?php
$sql = "SELECT product_id,product_name FROM products";

$result = mysqli_query($link, $sql);

$products = array();

while($row = mysqli_fetch_array($result)) {
    $products[] = $row;
}
mysqli_close($link);
?>
```

Finally, we have created a table of products with product name and options to edit/

delete products -

```php
<?php foreach($products as $product): ?>
    <tr>
        <td><?php echo $product["product_name"];?></td>
        <td><a href="edit.php?id=<?php echo $product["product_id"]; ?>">
                                    Edit</a></td>
        <td><a href="delete.php?id=<?php echo $product["product_id"]; ?
>">
                                    Delete</a></td>
    </tr>
<?php endforeach; ?>
```

As you can see, we have used a foreach loop to iterate through the products. We have used an alternative syntax of foreach loop, where we have started loop using the syntax -

```php
<?php foreach($products as $product): ?>
```

and then finally closed the loop with -

```php
<?php endforeach; ?>
```

This alternative syntax is more convenient while working with HTML. Inside the loop, we have created links to delete.php and edit.php pages using the product id. We have added a few lines of code in "e-commerce/admin/css/style.css" page to set alternative row colors of the products table -

```css
.products_table td {
    width: 160px;
    text-align: center;
}

.products_table tr:nth-child(even) {
    background-color:#33FF99;
}

.products_table tr:nth-child(odd) {
    background-color:#66CCFF;
}
```

Product Edit Page

Now let's create the edit.php page to handle the update of products. Once we click "Edit" link from our product management page, it will take us to the product update page with the existing product information already populated -

You can choose to keep the exiting product image which in that case, just leave the image upload box empty. Otherwise, select a new product image to replace old one.

Now, let's create "edit.php" page will the below code under the directory "e-commerce/admin" -

```php
<?php
require_once("db.connect.php");

$id = mysql_real_escape_string($_GET["id"]);

$sql = "SELECT * FROM products WHERE product_id=$id";

$result = mysqli_query($link, $sql);

$product = mysqli_fetch_array($result);

mysqli_close($link);
?>
```

```html
<html>
<head>
      <title>Update Product</title>
      <link rel="stylesheet" type="text/css" href="css/style.css"/>
</head>

<body>
      <div id="content">
            <h3>Update Product</h3>
            <form method="post" action="process_update.php"
enctype="multipart/form-data">
                  <input type="hidden" name="product_id" value="<?php echo
                                          $product["product_id"]; ?>"/>
            <table>
                  <tr>
                        <td>Product Name</td>
                        <td><input type="text" name="product_name" size="45"
                        value="<?php echo $product["product_name"]; ?>"/></
td>
                  </tr>
                  <tr>
                        <td>Product Description</td>
                        <td><textarea name="product_description" rows="10"
      cols="45"><?php echo $product["product_description"]; ?></textarea></td>
                  </tr>
                  <tr>
                        <td>Product Price</td>
                        <td><input type="text" name="product_price"
value="<?                          php echo $product["product_price"]; ?>"/
></td>
                  </tr>
                  <tr>
                        <td>Product Image (leave blank to keep existing
image)</td>
                        <td><input type="file" name="product_image"/></td>
                  </tr>
                  <tr>
                        <td>andnbsp;</td>
                        <td><input type="submit" value="Update Product"/></
```
210

```
td>
                    </tr>
            </table>
            </form>
        </div>
</body>
</html>
```

The PHP code block at the top of edit.php file gets the product id from $_GET array and then retrieves that product from the database. We then store the product information in a variable named $product.

```
<?php
require_once("db.connect.php");

$id = mysql_real_escape_string($_GET["id"]);

$sql = "SELECT * FROM products WHERE product_id=$id";

$result = mysqli_query($link, $sql);

$product = mysqli_fetch_array($result);

mysqli_close($link);
?>
```

The rest of the code of edit.php file should look familiar to you. They contain nearly identical code of add_product.php page but with the previous values of product already set to the form fields. Note however that we need to set the product id as a hidden form field -

```
<input type="hidden" name="product_id" value="<?php echo

    $product["product_id"]; ?>" />
```

The submission of this update form is handled by "process_update.php" page. Once you submit the product update page, it will look something like this -

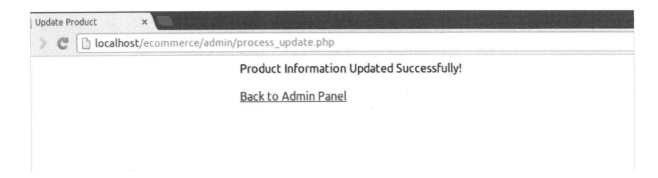

Let's create this "process_update.php" page under the "e-commerce/admin" directory -

```php
<?php
require_once("db.connect.php");

$product_id = mysql_real_escape_string($_POST["product_id"]);
$product_name = mysql_real_escape_string($_POST["product_name"]);
$product_description =
mysql_real_escape_string($_POST["product_description"]);
$product_price = mysql_real_escape_string($_POST["product_price"]);

$sql = "UPDATE products SET product_name = '$product_name',
                            product_description = '$product_description',
            product_price = '$product_price'";

//if image file is uploaded, then replace previous image
if(isset($_FILES["product_image"]["name"]) andand $_FILES["product_image"]
["error"] == 0) {
     $product_image = $_FILES["product_image"]["name"];

     //move the uploaded image to images directory
     move_uploaded_file($_FILES["product_image"]["tmp_name"],
                    "../images/". $_FILES["product_image"]["name"]);

     $sql .= ", product_image = '$product_image'";
}

$sql .= " WHERE product_id = $product_id";
?>

<html>
```

```
<head>
      <title>Update Product</title>
      <link rel="stylesheet" type="text/css" href="css/style.css"/>
</head>
<body>
      <div id="content">
      <?php
            if(mysqli_query($link, $sql)) {
                  echo "<p>Product Information Updated Successfully!</p>";
            }
            else {
                  echo mysqli_error($link);
            }
      ?>
      <p><a href="index.php">Back to Admin Panel</a></p>
      </div>
</body>
</html>
```

The above code should look familiar to you, so I will not explain it further except the UPDATE query part.

```
$sql = "UPDATE products SET product_name = '$product_name',
                        product_description = '$product_description',
            product_price = '$product_price'";

//if image file is uploaded, then replace previous image
if(isset($_FILES["product_image"]["name"]) andand $_FILES["product_image"]
["error"] == 0) {
      $product_image = $_FILES["product_image"]["name"];

      //move the uploaded image to images directory
      move_uploaded_file($_FILES["product_image"]["tmp_name"],
                        "../images/". $_FILES["product_image"]["name"]);

      $sql .= ", product_image = '$product_image'";
}

$sql .= " WHERE product_id = $product_id";
```

213

We have assigned the UPDATE query to the $sql variable. But initially, we have only declared a part of UPDATE query to $sql variable. This is because later, we will check if user has uploaded a new file or not. In the case that user has uploaded a new file, the code inside the 'if' block will be executed and the new file name will be added to the $sql query. Finall, we append the WHERE clause of the UPDATE query.

Product Delete Page

Next, we create the delete.php page under the "e-commerce/admin" directory which handles the deletion of products. The product management page (index.php) has a delete option where the product id is passed as query string to the delete.php page. If you click that delete link, the delete.php page will be executed and we want the corresponding product to be deleted from database. Let's see the code for delete.php page -

```php
<?php
require_once("db.connect.php");
$product_id = mysql_real_escape_string($_GET["id"]);
$sql = "DELETE FROM products WHERE product_id = $product_id";
mysqli_query($link, $sql);
header("Location: index.php");
?>
```

We can see that we first get the product id from $_GET array and then execute a DELETE command with that product id -

```php
$product_id = mysql_real_escape_string($_GET["id"]);
$sql = "DELETE FROM products WHERE product_id = $product_id";
mysqli_query($link, $sql);
```

Finally, we redirect to the index.php page using header() function -

```php
header("Location: index.php");
```

So now if you click any delete link from index.php page, that corresponding product will be removed from database.

With this delete page, our backend part of the e-commerce site is now done. Let's move onto the development of the frontend part of our website.

Frontend Development

We will now start building the frontend portion of our e-commerce website. We will start with the frontend home page which is the index.php page.

Frontend Home Page

Our frontend home page will have a list of available products with the option to buy those items. At the top of the page, a user will be able to see the number of items currently in their shopping cart. It will look something like this -

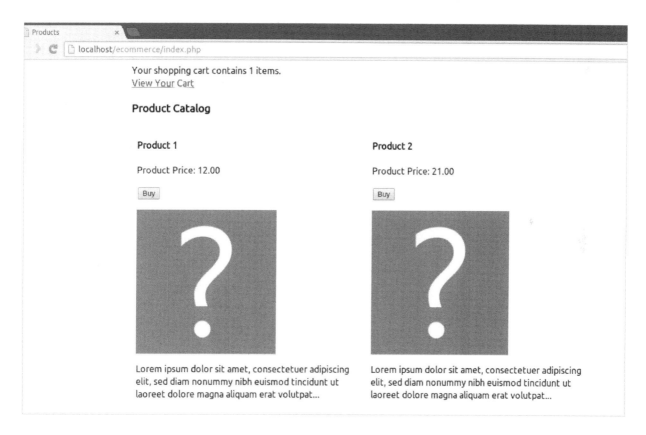

You can see a "Buy" button beside every product in our product catalog. If the user clicks the buy button, that product will be added to their shopping cart. The "View Your Cart" link at the top of the product catalog will show the products currently added to their shopping cart (and will have the option to checkout etc).

Now let's see the code of the above page. Create a new page called "index.php" under the directory "e-commerce" with the following code -

```php
<?php
session_start();
if(!isset($_SESSION["cart"])) {
    $_SESSION["cart"] = array();
}

if(isset($_POST["submit"])) {
    $_SESSION["cart"][] = $_POST["product_id"];
}
?>

<html>
<head>
    <title>Products</title>
    <link rel="stylesheet" type="text/css" href="css/style.css"/>
</head>
<body>
    <div id="content">
        <p>
            Your shopping cart contains <?php echo

count($_SESSION["cart"]) ?> items.<br/>
            <a href="cart.php">View Your Cart</a>
        </p>

        <?php require_once("catalog.php"); ?>
    </div>
</body>
</html>
```

Let's go through the code of the above index.php file.

```php
session_start();
if(!isset($_SESSION["cart"])) {
    $_SESSION["cart"] = array();
}
```

The index.php file starts with this portion of code. Here, we first start the session (using session_start() function call) and then check if a session variable named

$_SESSION["cart"] is set or not. In case the mentioned session variable isn't set yet, we then set that session variable and initialize with an empty array.

```php
if(isset($_POST["submit"])) {
    $_SESSION["cart"][] = $_POST["product_id"];
}
```

The above code block checks if the variable $_POST["submit"] is set or not. Remember the "Buy" button beside every product in our product catalog? Once the user clicks such a button, that product id will be passed as $_POST array data and we then add that product id to the $_SESSION["cart"] array. This is how a particular product is added to a user's shopping cart.

```php
<p>
   Your shopping cart contains <?php echo count($_SESSION["cart"]) ?
>items.<br/>
   <a href="cart.php">View Your Cart</a>
</p>
```

The first line of code shows the item count of their shopping cart while the second line has a link to view the user's shopping cart.

```php
<?php require_once("catalog.php"); ?>
```

This line includes another PHP file, catalog.php, where the code for product catalog is written. We will see the code of catalog.php shortly.

This index.php file also reference a CSS file. Create a new CSS file named "style.css" under "e-commerce/css" with the following content -

```css
#content {
    width: 850px;
    margin:0 auto;
}

tr:nth-child(even) {
    background-color:#33FF99;
}

tr:nth-child(odd) {
```

```css
        background-color:#66CCFF;
}

tr:nth-child(1) {
        background-color:#6666FF;
}

.product {
        width: 400px;
        float: left;
        margin-right: 10px;
}
```

Now let's see the code for catalog.php file. Create a file named "catalog.php" under the directory "e-commerce" with the following code -

```php
<?php
require_once("admin/db.connect.php");

$sql = "SELECT * FROM products";

$result = mysqli_query($link, $sql);

$products = array();

while($row = mysqli_fetch_array($result)) {
        $products[] = $row;
}

mysqli_close($link);
?>

<h3>Product Catalog</h3>

<?php foreach($products as $product): ?>
<div class="product">
        <h4><?php echo $product["product_name"];?></h4>
        <p>
                Product Price: <?php echo $product["product_price"];?>
                <form method="post" action="">
```

218

```
                <input type="hidden" name="product_id" value="<?php echo
$product["product_id"]; ?>"/>
                    <input type="submit" name="submit" value="Buy"/>
            </form>
        </p>
        <img src="http://localhost/e-commerce/images/<?php echo
$product["product_image"]; ?>" width="250" height="250"/>
        <p><?php echo $product["product_description"];?></p>
    </div>
<?php endforeach; ?>
```

The PHP code block at the beginning of the "catalog.php" simply retrieves all products from table and stores them in an array called $products. We will later loop through that array to create our product catalog.

```
<img src="http://localhost/e-commerce/images/<?php echo
$product["product_image"]; ?>" width="250" height="250"/>
```

Notice how we get the product images. When uploading images, we store image files to the "e-commerce/images" directory and also store the image file names into the database table. Using these two informations, we generate the image src dynamically.

```
<form method="post" action="">
    <input type="hidden" name="product_id" vlaue="<?php
                            echo $product["product_id"]; ?>"/>
    <input type="submit" name="submit" value="Buy"/>
</form>
```

Within each iteration of the loop, we embed this form with the product id passed as a hidden form field and a submit button labeled "Buy". This form has a method of "post" and an empty action which means that the form will be submitted to the same PHP file which will hold the form code.

In our case, since we include this catalog.php file from index.php file, this form will be submitted to index.php file. We have already seen the code that will handle this form submission and add product to user's shopping cart.

For database connectivity, this catalog.php file includes the "db.connect.php" file, which we previously created in our "e-commerce/admin" directory -

```php
require_once("admin/db.connect.php");
```

Now you can see how the products are added to user's shopping cart. Next we will see how users can view their shopping cart.

Shopping Cart

First, let's see how our shopping cart will look like -

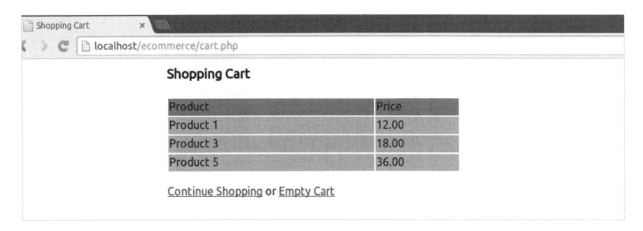

In addition to showing the products currently in our shopping list, this page will have option to continue shopping (which will take us to index.php page) and we will also have an option to empty our shopping cart.

If the cart has no item, then it will look like this -

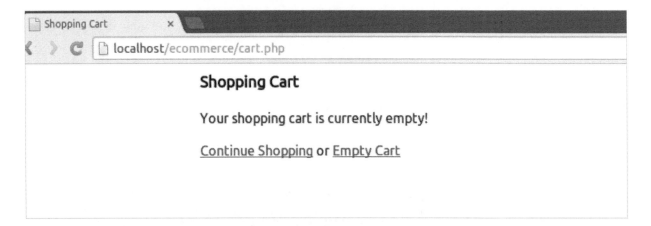

Now let's create a new PHP file called "cart.php" under the directory "e-commerce" with the following code -

```php
<?php
session_start();
$cart = $_SESSION["cart"];

if(count($cart) > 0) {
    require_once("admin/db.connect.php");

    $sql = "SELECT * FROM products WHERE product_id IN
(".implode(",",                                 $cart).")";

    $result = mysqli_query($link, $sql);

    $products = array();

    while($row = mysqli_fetch_array($result)) {
        $products[] = $row;
    }

    mysqli_close($link);
}
?>

<html>
<head>
    <title>Shopping Cart</title>
    <link rel="stylesheet" type="text/css" href="css/style.css" />
</head>
<body>
    <div id="content">
    <h3>Shopping Cart</h3>
    <?php if(count($cart) == 0): ?>
        <p>Your shopping cart is currently empty!</p>
    <?php else: ?>
        <table>
            <tr>
                <td width="25%">Product</td>
                <td width="10%">Price</td>
            </tr>
            <?php foreach($products as $product): ?>
            <tr>
```

```
                <td><?php echo $product["product_name"];?></td>
                <td><?php echo $product["product_price"];?></td>
            </tr>
            <?php endforeach; ?>
        </table>
    <?php endif; ?>
    <p>
        <a href="index.php">Continue Shopping</a> or
        <a href="empty_cart.php">Empty Cart</a>
    </p>
    </div>
</body>
</html>
```

Let's step through the code of this file.

```
session_start();
$cart = $_SESSION["cart"];
```

First, we retrieve the session data stored previously and assign that to $cart variable. The $cart variable will contain an array of product ids.

```
if(count($cart) > 0)
```

In the above code, we check the item count of $cart array. If it has at least one item, we will perform a database query to get the corresponding products which have id stored in $cart array.

```
$sql = "SELECT * FROM products WHERE product_id IN (".implode(",",
    $cart).")";
```

The above is the SQL query to get the products from database which are in the user's shopping cart. We have used the PHP implode() function to get a comma separated string of product ids. So if the $cart contains the product id of 1,2 and 5, the **implode(",",$cart)** will return the string "1,2,5". In that case, the above $sql query will be -
```
$sql = "SELECT * FROM products WHERE product_id IN (1,2,5)";
```

Note that we have used the IN keyword within our WHERE clause. This will retrieve the products that have id of 1,2 or 5.

```php
<?php if(count($cart) == 0): ?>
```

The above checks if our shopping cart has any item or not. In case it does not have any item, we simply show the user a message. Otherwise, we show the products in the user's shopping cart.

```html
<a href="index.php">Continue Shopping</a> or
<a href="empty_cart.php">Empty Cart</a>
```

At the bottom of "cart.php" file, there are two links. The first one takes the user to index.php page to select more items. The second link empties the shopping cart.

Emptying the Shopping Cart

Create a new PHP file named "empty_cart.php" under the directory "e-commerce" with the following code -

```php
<?php
session_start();
session_unset($_SESSION["cart"]);
header("Location: index.php");
?>
```

Once the user clicks the "Empty Cart" link from the cart.php page, this page will be called and this page will simply unset the $_SESSION["cart"]. As a result, the user's shopping cart will be emptied. The user is next redirected to index.php page.

What we have done so far?

This is just a recap of what we have done so far -

- We have started creating the database and products table.
- We have built the backend of the website. From the backend of the website, we can add a new product, update an existing product and remove a product.
- In the frontend of the website, we have created a product catalog page where users can add products to their shopping cart.
- User can view their shopping carts and also empty their carts.

These are the functions we have built so far for our e-commerce website. We have covered the fundamental principles of building such a website. Note though that we are still some distance away from building a fully functional e-commerce website. For that, we need some other advanced skills that aren't taught in this beginner level book. The main target of this e-commerce project example was to give you a sense of how different pieces fit together in the context of web development. After reading all the chapters of the book and following this example project, you should feel comfortable to adopt any advanced resource to keep learning more and building more cool stuffs.

What to Do Next?

In this section, we will see what else you can do to improve the ongoing e-commerce project and add more features to it. Unlike previous sections, I will not go through the details of these features, rather I will try to give some guidelines which you can follow and point you to other resources for further study.

User Login System

You can provide your users the ability to register and login. For this task, you will need to create a new table in your database to store information about the users. You will have to build a registration form, which will give an interface to the users to enter their information. When they submit the registration form, the corresponding processing PHP script will create an user account with those information.

You will also need to create a login form for the users to login with their username and password they entered while creating their account. You will find plenty of resources online about how to do these tasks. One of the good and easy to follow tutorial link is provided below -

http://code.tutsplus.com/tutorials/user-membership-with-php--net-1523

Payment Processing

After the product is added to a user's shopping cart, they will expect to have a checkout page where they can proceed to payment. PayPal is the most widely used method for handling online payments. They provide their own API (Application Programming Interface) for processing payments easily. The official Paypal Developer website contains all the information you need -

https://developer.paypal.com/

There are other payment processors as well. For example, to handle credit card processing, you can check the following resources -

Authorize.net - http://www.authorize.net/
2Checkout - https://www.2checkout.com/
Stripe - https://stripe.com/

Below are the links of some of the tutorials you will find useful to implement payment processing to your website -

http://code.tutsplus.com/tutorials/creating-a-paypal-payment-form--net-6

http://code.tutsplus.com/tutorials/how-to-process-credit-cards-with-paypal-payments-pro-using-php--net-25397

http://code.tutsplus.com/tutorials/so-you-want-to-accept-credit-cards-online--net-25457

Other Improvements

You can add a number of other improvements to your e-commerce project, like adding product categories, building a product search functionality, create individual product page, give product recommendation to users and many other features. Given you have the basics under your belt and lots of excellent free resources over the web, you will be able to make these improvements. A list of resources are provided at the end of Chapter 15, so don't stop here, rather keep learning more advanced and cool stuffs.

Printed in Great Britain
by Amazon